D1617069

The wolves are coming back

Manchester University Press

The wolves are coming back

The politics of fear in Eastern Germany

Rebecca Pates and Julia Leser

Manchester University Press

Published by Manchester University Press
Altrincham Street, Manchester M1 7JA
www.manchesteruniversitypress.co.uk

British Library Cataloguing-in-Publication Data
A catalogue record for this book is available from the British Library

ISBN 978 1 5261 4701 1 hardback

First published 2021

Typeset by Servis Filmsetting Ltd, Stockport, Cheshire
Printed in Great Britain by Bell & Bain Ltd, Glasgow

Contents

List of figures

List of figures

Preface

South of Leipzig where this book was written, just at the edge of the Auwald forest, the *flâneuse* trying to escape the bustle of the city stumbles upon a curious monument: a stone wolf erected on a plinth with an inscription that reads: 'The last wolves were sighted here in 1720'. At that time and until the late nineteenth century, the wolf was a serious competitor for local farmers, and the animal's extinction was apparently worth a monument. Today, three hundred years later, the wolves are returning to German territories, and it is a problem: not because the returning predators pose a serious threat to humans objectively but because the wolf has become a cypher of political agitation and outrage that goes hand in hand with the politics of fear central to the rising nationalism in Eastern Germany. Amidst the turmoil of the rise of the far right and the crisis of democracy, the wolf today is a metaphor for what is going on in Eastern German politics.

The wolf has always been a popular protagonist of folk imaginaries and a central metaphor in fairy tales, mythology, religion and political theory. Until the end of the nineteenth century, popular stories about the 'big bad wolf' seemed to correlate with the widespread wish to exterminate the predators that supposedly killed entire flocks of sheep. In fairy tales such as *Little Red Hiding Hood*, the wolf symbolises impending disaster, menacing evil and existential threat. The wolf stands for the dark side of nature, serving as a boundary object between the safety of civilisation and a hostile, threatening, uncontrollable and libidinous nature. For centuries, the wolf has served as a culturally anchored metaphor of fear, and, as such, has found entry into modern conceptions of politics. As we shall see again later, Thomas Hobbes famously argued that man himself is wolf to man – *homo homini lupus* – unless civilisation intervenes. The wolf, then, is part and parcel of a dualism between good and evil nature, between order and chaos, civilisation and barbarism — and a metaphor for the damage that people do to each other. So even though, in a literal sense, the wolf is no threat other than to sheep or deer, as an anthropomorphic object the wolf becomes accessible to political discourse.

The invocation of the returning wolf as an object of fear in far-right politics is thus a powerful strategy. Styled by populist right-wing actors as an 'invasive species' that does not belong here and poses an existential threat to 'our women and children', the wolf evokes and resonates with anti-immigration sentiments and widespread fears of demographic catastrophe. In Eastern Germany the returning wolves have easily claimed new territories for themselves, which they found within extensive renatured areas that tell of thirty years of structural changes, massive deindustrialisation and depopulation processes that amount to the loss of two generations.

A British radio journalist, Trevor Dann, asked one of us in February 2018 during a workshop at Cambridge University: 'What is going on that can explain the rise of the far right

Preface

in Eastern Germany?' *The Wolves Are Coming Back* is one answer to that question. For the wolves have been returning for three reasons that are closely connected to the transformations that have been affecting the political life in Eastern Germany for three decades. First, Nature is rebounding. Eastern Germany had been devastated by heavy industries turning rivers blue, the sky grey and the population sick. In the course of the last thirty years, a great deal of the environmental degradation has been reversed: there is just much more nature to come back to. Second, walls have come down between Germany and Poland. With the lack of border guards and fences, animals can move more freely, and wolves have roamed westwards. Third, *de*population has rapidly accelerated since the end of the GDR. Even towns have been shrinking. Many medium-sized and large towns have lost a considerable segment of their population since the 1990s. So, wolves have come back. But with modernisation of industry, including of agriculture, and with the privatisation of formally commonly held land, many traditional rural occupations are waning. The predator thus acts as a cipher for change, but also for globalisation and migration, for environmental politics that harm 'the little man', for the perception of a Western German colonising. This book, which covers events up to 21 May 2020, is an attempt to explain the rise of the far right in Eastern Germany through the lens of the returning wolves, while moving beyond stereotypic representations of 'the East' and shining a light on the complexities of post-socialist life and losses.

Acknowledgements

The authors would like to thank Pauline Betche, Anna Bentzien and Ronja Morgenthaler for giving us permission to quote from their interviews. They would also like to thank Pauline Betche for fact-checking, Ariane Kolden and Lena-Marie Schmidt for editorial help, and Mario Futh and Birgit Ruß for taking on a great number of administrative tasks, keeping our desks free for a summer. Ariane Kolden did additional research for this book. Trevor Dann and BBC Radio 4 are to be thanked for letting us develop the idea of *wolves coming back* for a documentary on Eastern German politics in November 2018, thus providing an occasion to develop some of the ideas we then used for writing this book. This radio documentary led Jonathan de Peyer from Manchester University Press to approach the authors with an idea for this book, and we are highly indebted to him for his support throughout the process of writing it.

Parts of this book have been shared at the 26th International Conference of Europeanists – *Sovereignties in Contention: Nations, Regions and Citizens in Europe* in Madrid in 2019, at the European Conference of Politics & Gender in Amsterdam in 2019, at the *Beyond Identity? New Avenues for Interdisciplinary Research* Workshop, organised by

Acknowledgements

the Academia Europaea Wroclaw Knowledge Hub & Willy Brandt Centre for German and European Studies at Wroclaw University in 2019, at the *Die politisierte Gesellschaft? Politik, Emotion und Protest* Conference, organised by Deutsche Nachwuchsgesellschaft für Politik- und Sozialwissenschaft in Hannover in 2019, and at the *Vorstellungen von Gemeinschaft und Nation im Kontextgegenwärtiger rechtspopulistischer Mobilisierungen* Symposium, organised by the International Psychoanalytic University in Berlin in 2020.

Parts of Chapter 2 are developed in a longer article, 'Performing "resistance" – the far right's master narrative' in *The Journal of Culture* 8(1), 13–21, authored by Julia Leser, Florian Spissinger, Jamela Homeyer and Tobias Neidel. Chapter 5 includes material from the article 'The functionality of affects. Conceptualizing far-right populist politics beyond negative emotions' in *Global Discourse* 10(2), 325–342, by Julia Leser and Florian Spissinger. In this regard we would like to thank Florian Spissinger, Jamela Stratenwerth, Tobias Neidel and Paul Lissner for their valuable input and feedback.

Finally, we wish to thank all the colleagues and friends at Leipzig University where we have been fortunate to teach and conduct our research while writing this book. And most importantly, we are immensely grateful to Stephan Kaasche, who helped us understand the many dimensions of the wolf problem, and even took us to the vast and empty landscapes of Lusatia to find actual wolves, though in the end, they eluded our curious gaze.

List of abbreviations

AfD	Alternative für Deutschland (Alternative for Germany, political party)
CDU	Christlich Demokratische Union Deutschlands (Christian Democratic Union, political party)
DM	Deutsche Mark (German Mark, pre-Euro currency in Western Germany)
FDP	Freie Demokratische Partei (Free Democratic Party, political party)
GDL	German Defence League (anti-Islamic political organisation, since 2010)
GDR	German Democratic Republic (Eastern Germany 1949–89)
HOGESA	Hooligans against Salafism (right-wing anti-Muslim movement, since 2014)
IfS	Institut für Staatspolitik (Institute for State Politics, right-wing think tank since 2000)
LPG	Landwirtschaftliche Produktionsgenossenschaft (state-run agricultural co-op, a collectivised farm in the GDR)

List of abbreviations

MfS	Ministerium für Staatssicherheit (Ministry for State Security, commonly known as Stasi)
MP	Member of Parliament
NPD	Nationaldemokratische Partei Deutschlands (National Democratic Party of Germany, political party)
NSDAP	Nationalsozialistische Deutsche Arbeiterpartei (National Socialist German Workers' Party, political party 1920–45)
NSU	Nationalsozialistischer Untergrund (National Socialist Underground, Eastern German terrorist group 1999–2011)
PEGIDA	Patriotische Europäer gegen die Islamisierung des Abendlandes (Patriotic Europeans against the Islamisation of the Occident, since 2014)
PI	Politically Incorrect (Right-wing blog, since 2004)
THÜGIDA	Thüringen gegen die Islamisierung des Abendlandes (Thuringia against the Islamisation of the Occident, right-wing political movement 2015–17)

Introduction:
Wolf politics

The great transformation brings us mass murder, rape to an
extent never known before, the brutalisation of our society,
and the wolf experiment brings us damages to the tune of
hundreds of thousands of Euros.

AfD MP Karsten Hilse in an address
to the German Bundestag in 2019[1]

Homo homini lupus?
Hunting predators and the politics of belonging

On a cold January evening in 2019 we find ourselves driving through Lusatia, a region in eastern Saxony spanning
into Brandenburg and western Poland. This region is home
to the Sorbs, one of the four officially recognised German
national minorities. Lusatia is also home to a rising number
of wolf packs. In the spring of 2019, 73 wolf packs and 30
wolf pairs roam the north-east of Germany, their territory
extending from the Polish to the Danish borders. Along
with wolves and Sorbs, what Lusatia has to offer besides
beautiful pine forests, glacial sand dunes and renatured
areas reminiscent of the former brown coal industrial complex are beautiful medieval and Renaissance towns. These
include Hoyerswerda, Bautzen and Görlitz, where endemic

right-wing attacks on visible minorities, refugees and left-wing youth, arson attacks on refugee shelters and vociferous anti-establishmentarian political splinter parties have of late gained the attention of the national press. None of this is visible as we drive through the dark and deserted landscapes on this winter evening. All we see in the headlights of our car are narrow empty roads meandering through forests and fields. Just before we reach our destination, we are startled by four gleaming eyes from a couple of deer staring at the approaching car from the side of the road.

Our destination that night is the Gaststätte zur Grafschaft, a German inn in Neudorf Klösterlich near Wittichenau. Neudorf Klösterlich is home to about eighty people and its inn has a reputation for serving an outstanding venison stew. We are here at the invitation of the Blue Party, which invited Lusatians to a public hearing concerning the wolf. We find the inn traditionally furnished with wooden chairs and tables, embroidered tablecloths and wooden beams, and ourselves a little out of place. The waiter offers us seats in a corner, well away from the well attended centre table at which farmers, hunters and small business operators concur that the wolf is a significant problem, and its defenders at best bloody-minded opponents of the rural population.

The Blue Party is reaching out to rural voters – like the other new nationalist parties – and takes a clear position towards large predators: They have no place in German territory as they endanger 'our' way of life. The dentist who organised a petition with some 18,600 signatures in favour of regulating the wolf population is present, as is the spokesman of a citizens' initiative for 'wolf victims and worried citizens' (Bürgerinitiative 'Wolfsgeschädigte/besorgte Bürger'), a sometime speaker at Patriotic Europeans against the Islamisation of the Occident (Patriotische Europäer gegen die Islamisierung des Abendlandes, PEGIDA) rallies and the odd local farmer seeking to protect their sheep, as well as various hunters. The evening's host, the Saxon MP Kirsten Muster (Blue Party), is giving a number of dispassionately presented legal arguments.[2] Since 1990, the wolf has been a protected species in Germany; killing a wolf has become a crime punishable by a sentence of imprisonment of up to five years. Still, the MP's presentation goes, these wolves are not Saxon wolves, or even German ones, but rather western Polish ones. As migrants, she explains, they do not deserve our protection, they do not belong here, they are invaders of our territory, threatening the local way of life. She argues that they are not even *real* wolves but merely impure hybrids – the offspring of wolves that have mixed with the local canine population – and thus undeserving of being lawfully protected.

The audience does not take kindly to this presentation. No objection is made to the arguments as such – no one cares about legal arguments. For who decided that German law or even EU law applies to this region? 'We are the people', 'This is a democracy, and we don't want wolves!' are statements often repeated this evening. The wolf is pro-tected, they feel, by the establishment, by Brussels, by Berlin and, in particular, by those Greens who are also in favour of other types of dangerous immigrants threatening our way of life, threatening our women and children, threatening our very existence. Nobody has asked us, they complain, and we just don't want to live with the wolf breathing down our necks as we go about our business. For them, the wolf, like the refugees centrally allocated to cities, towns and villages all over Germany, has been a problem and nobody seems to be doing anything about it. And in fact, smallholders and sheep farmers are having considerable problems keeping afloat, and professional shepherds, especially peripatetic shepherds, are becoming ever rarer; so lambs and ewes being killed don't help those small businesses survive, and though it's as often as not ravens that kill the lambs on the fields, the wolf is used to bring the point home that shepherds are losing their livelihoods.[3]

A man introducing himself as Dr Manfred Habert*,[4] the local aquaculture tsar, stands up: 'We're against the settlement of wolves in Saxony and Germany,' as the audience approvingly knocks on the tables, 'and we want to shoot the wolf as we used to in the GDR! We didn't miss anything in the GDR! We didn't have problems with our sheep, or with our wildlife population, and we weren't afraid of going into the forest! Now we reached a situation that is no longer bearable, and you come here proposing some small legal changes. You won't get any votes from the people present here tonight!' He sits down, to the applause of the room. And so it goes on, many repeat that the GDR was more democratic and refreshingly wolf-less. Finally, one of the few women attending the event stands up and introduces herself as a local farmer who owns a couple of sheep: 'I'm just a stupid peasant. But I love my sheep! You might say, I like to eat my sheep, too, just like the wolf, but when *I* kill the sheep, it's with respect. Wolves do not respect my sheep, they cause carnage. It's the Greens, they got the wolves to come, they want to kill us all, with wolves, with refugees ...' Her point made, her voice faltering, she adds quietly, vengefully: 'I think they should be shot, too.' And Engelbert Merz, the PEGIDA speaker, suggests: 'Let's send those wolves to the Greens, let's catch them, put them in cages, and send them straight to those people in the cities who like wolves.'

The rural population in Lusatia, the sheep farmers, small business operators and local dignitaries, hunters, the mushroom foragers and the parents whose children have to wait for school buses in the late winter dawn, have to bear the consequences of what the distant, wolf-unaffected people living in cities, the Green party, the elites, the romantic wolf lovers and the even more distant decision-makers in Brussels have agreed upon. That is one side of the complaint. But the underlying logics why the wolf does not belong ring a familiar tune. The trope of the wolf in this argument reminds us of the AfD manifesto that states, 'Islam does not belong in Germany'. Wolves and immigrants, in the populist arguments, share the negative qualities of bringing no benefit, incurring costs to the locals, including potential physical harm to women, whilst simply belonging elsewhere. According to the far-right ethnoplural-ist narrative, there are areas in which Muslims belong, and it is not Europe. There are areas in which wolves belong too, and it is not here.

After the stabbing of a man in Chemnitz in 2018, André Poggenburg tweeted that the 'mass migration' to Germany would turn into a 'knife migration' (*Messermigration*). Markus Frohnmaier, AfD member of the Bundestag, tweeted on the night of the Chemnitz pogroms: 'If the state fails at protecting its citizens, people go to the streets to protect themselves! It is that simple. The citizens are obligated to stop the death-bringing knife migration.'[5] Years ago, in 2015, Marcus Pretzell, former AfD member, then member of the Blue Party and husband of former AfD member Frauke Petry, argued in an interview with the newspaper *Kölner Express*: 'The arming of the border police only makes sense if the officers are allowed to use their weapons in case of emergency – to warn, to hurt, and potentially, to kill.'[6] And in the recently leaked report on the AfD by the Federal Office for the Protection of the Constitution (Bundesamt für

Verfassungsschutz), a 2018 Facebook post by the AfD district chapter Erzgebirge is quoted: 'When hundreds of aggressive Africans are storming a few border control officers, while waving flame-throwers and throwing quicklime, then the use of live ammunition should be appropriate for reasons of self-defence alone.'[7] According to their narratives: Muslims kill. Wolves kill. And we don't need either population here. We are civilised, they are feral.

In German fairy tales, the wolf is always initially dangerous but vanquished by a hunter: it stands for a fight of civilisation versus barbarism, organised village life versus predatory invaders, peace and prosperity versus death and destitution. In fairy tales such as *Little Red Riding Hood* or *The Wolf and the Seven Young Goats*, the wolf is always a predator, but, unlike the human hunter in the story, one that acts in accordance with instinct rather than order and civilisation. But the wolf is always a rival to the civilised hunter, and, as such, a rival in the metaphors of untamed and natural versus established and civilised order. As an untamed male figure, the wolf also stands for predation against women, as Charles Perrault noted at the end of his version of the tale:

> Moral: Children, especially attractive, well bred young ladies, should never talk to strangers, for if they should do so, they may well provide dinner for a wolf. I say 'wolf,' but there are various kinds of wolves. There are also those who are charming, quiet, polite, unassuming, complacent, and sweet, who pursue young women at home and in the streets. And unfortunately, it is these gentle wolves who are the most dangerous ones of all.[8]

The story of *Little Red Riding Hood* thus involves a rapist wolf, and this is a trope reiterated with a twist in a debate in the Bundestag in 2019, when an AfD MP argues that the return of the wolf is part and parcel of the sort of politics that lead to the rape and pillaging of the Germans by migrants. In his speech to the Bundestag, the AfD politician Karsten Hilse rises to elaborate on his party's motion:

> The biggest problem is that it is an irresponsible experiment of great consequence to introduce a large predator whose native habitat is sparsely populated by humans into a region that is in fact densely populated. Everybody involved must be fully aware of the potential consequences. And nobody – nobody! – gave you the right to conduct this experiment! Just as with the great transformation, the consequences are out of control. The great transformation brings us mass murder, rape to an extent never known before, the brutalisation of our society, and the wolf experiment brings us damages to the tune of hundreds of thousands of Euros. [...] And the Left-Green block of dreamers stick to the status quo of wolf politics; the wolf is *the* to-be-worshipped holy animal. [...] However, what does the affected rural population say? What does the livestock owner do when the big bad wolf (*Isegrim*) has repeatedly haunted his premises, when he finds his pasturage in the morning with his sheep barely alive, their bellies ripped open, their intestines oozing out, or their hind legs chewed on? He takes action. If a government leaves their people alone with their worries and commits a thousand-fold breaking of laws in regard to refugee and migration politics, then inhibitions are lowered, and people will take things into their own hands.[9]

As Hilse argues – accompanied by shouts of protest from the seats of the left and Green factions – the wolf problem is similar to the issue of immigration in that both problems are ignored by 'Left-Green daydreamers'. He accuses the Green party of being blindly favourable to the cultural benefits of migration and the natural benefits of wolves, working towards the 'great transformation', a term that refers to a conspiracy theory according to which local European populations are to be replaced by more compliant African and Muslim people.

By pursuing this argument the AfD is claiming that the well-established left and Green parties of the cosmopolitan, queer-, feminist- and animal-rights-focused urbanites have lost touch with the 'real' people, neither listening to nor recognising the needs of the rural population or riding roughshod over their needs. Thus, wolf politics lend themselves to a form of populism by promising to represent the *Volk*, the transcendental and biological unity that shares a unity of destiny.[10] As the man who rose to speak first at the Blue Party's citizen forum in Neudorf Klösterlich put it: 'Why did nobody ask us what we think about the wolf?' In the political debate the AfD makes use of and construes these objects of fear in order to reveal, in their opinion, the failure of the left and the Green parties, the failure of party politics and the failure of democracy. At the end of the Blue Party's evening of wolf politics in that remote inn, Engelbert Merz stood up again, precisely defining who he thought the people were: 'I am the sovereign! And I want wolves shot!' To which, quietly, the feted local dentist who had organised the petition that argued for regulating the wolves told us after the meeting: 'He's West German. Always loud, always important. Don't mistake him for one of us.' The people, after all, is a flexible category.

Wolves, then, stand for something other than canine predators; the discussion over wolves is a discussion about the very nature of representation, over the rules that govern public speaking, over the composition of German society and the role of the East Germans within it. In this book we would like to answer a number of questions. Why is the wolf – an animal that has not eaten or attacked a human in hundreds of years – given this role? Why are the new right-wing and nationalist parties emerging all over Eastern Germany so successfully, and are so much more successful than in the West? Furthermore, the Bundestag speech by Karsten Hilse provides an occasion to see how the wolf trope functions in political rhetoric. First, in inserting the migrant into an anti-wolf argument, Hilse's focus on the wolf as a frenzied killer – leaving *our* animals to die in agony ('bellies ripped apart, intestines oozing out') – contributes to the dehumanisation of migrants, making them appear even more dangerous, and even more alien, non-German, non-human and not-belonging. According to Hilse's logic, refugees *are* wolves, and responsible for 'mass murder', 'rape to an extent not known before' and 'the brutalisation of our society'. Thus, the 'wolf crisis' is not a successor to the 2015 'refugee crisis' but, according to the AfD discourse, it is a useful and almost necessary addition to the 'refugee crisis'. The endlessly repeated references to bloodthirsty wolves and raping migrants fuel an atmosphere of fear: The wolf is fuel spilled into the fire. Thus, the wolf complements and interweaves with the construed threat of a generic 'other'. Germany's current wolf politics led by populist parties such as the AfD reveal the arbitrariness of objects of fear in populist discourse.

In this study of the wolf as it features in current German right-wing politics, we are sketching a *folkish imaginary*, not because the wolf is a ubiquitous and dangerous animal, nor because it features particularly largely in the current politics of Germany; but because the wolf even as an innocent object helps to 'shed light on wider ideological structures'.[11] Not a single person has been killed or harmed by a wolf in centuries on German territory. Still, the return of the wolves to Germany has turned into an important problem, first and foremost in the sphere of discourse that overshadows political life in some rural communities,

Figure 0.1 Graffiti on a bus stop in Saxony, 'Wolf plague – Vote AfD!'

particularly in more remote regions of Brandenburg, Saxony and Mecklenburg-Vorpommern (see Figures 0.1 and 0.2). The trope of returning wolves resonates with a politics of fear by populist parties such as the AfD. As the linguist Ruth Wodak explains, 'such parties successfully construct fear and – related to the various real or imagined dangers – propose scapegoats that are blamed for threatening or actually damaging our societies'.[12] The mobilisation of fear is an effective strategic tool in political rhetoric; it turns migrants and refugees into presumed Islamist fanatics and terrorists, into knife murderers and rapists – irrespective of the fact that the crime statistics have actually decreased; it turns wolves into frenzied killers of livestock, of children, of ourselves – irrespective of the fact that no wolf has killed a person in Germany in two centuries.[13]

Figure 0.2 Overwritten graffiti on bus stop.

Wolves, then, are something that is feared, and as such to be evaluated according to whether they are *our wolves* or *their wolves*. The wolves that these rural inhabitants in our meeting want to shoot, then, are determinedly referred to as foreign, more specifically as Polish, as the meeting took place on the Polish border. Though on the Danish border, Danish wolves have been reported in German media – a genetic analysis has shown, however, that many 'Danish wolves' in Germany are descendants of a 'German wolf' that had made its way to Denmark.[14] The emphasis on the foreignness of the wolf population is then a function of what the speaker feels about wolves. Fans of the wolves refer to wolves having come back, implying that they are indigenous to the territory and are remigrating. But those who fear the wolf represent them as foreign, and represent those environmentalists supporting wolves as supporting the wrong side. The crisis of fear is a feature of the crisis of representation.

The wolves are returning to Germany, while German politics are transforming. The right-wing Alternative for Germany is now the third biggest party in the German parliament. It draws much of its support from places that have been referred to as the 'post-traumatic places' in Eastern Germany, structured by realities of disownment, disfranchisement and a lack of political representation. With right-wing populist parties being on the rise everywhere in Europe, politicians, journalists and scholars have become dedicated to diagnosing a crisis of democracy. With this book we offer an in-depth perspective on the theme of democracy in crisis through the prism of wolf politics in early twenty-first-century Eastern Germany. Investigating fringe political movements, the political agitation against both migrants and wolves, the perspectives of Eastern German hunters, farmers, rioters and self-appointed saviours of the nation, the book attempts to move beyond easy stereotypes and explanations and unravel the deep story of why Eastern German politics is shifting to the right.[15] The returning wolves serve both as metaphor and analytical tool to further an understanding of the logics and sentiments that underlie the rise of the right in Eastern German politics.

Wolf *demos*, or, Who is the crisis of democracy?

The crisis of representation is a fundamental flaw in representative democracy: as Georg Wilhelm Friedrich Hegel pointed out, some people fall outside the logics of representations, the very rich and the rabble (*Pöbel*). Neither group contributes to the general good by working. Thus, the bourgeoisie can present itself as uniquely contributing to the general good, and as uniquely positioned to govern for the good of the many. Considering this background, as the German political scientist Philip Manow has argued, the current insurrection can be read as one in which the rabble insists on taking the promises of representation seriously, and thus undermining the unspoken basis of a functioning representative democracy that is always already exclusionary.[16] This crisis in representation leads to a diagnosis that we are 'witnessing the worldwide rejection of liberal democracy and its replacement by some sort of populist authoritarianism', as Arjun Appadurai argues, pointing toward a widespread conception that places populism outside of democracy – more precisely, populism as a kind of 'constitutive other' to democracy.[17]

If populism is opposed to and a threat to democracy, then a fight against populist movements seems to be a pressing consequence: we need to stop them,[18] or we will see the rise of 'illiberal democracies', as Yascha Mounk argued in his book *The People vs. Democracy: Why Our Freedom Is in Danger and How to Save It*.[19] Other authors have argued that populism might be seen not necessarily as a threat to democracies but either as inherent to democracy, or even beneficial to democratic processes: Chantal Mouffe, for example, has argued that populism can be grasped as a necessary political resource of partisan character, able to redefine democratic politics as we know it.[20] From ethnographic empirical research we know how citizens' trust in democracy – or, more precisely, in democratic institutions – is currently eroding. In her study *Strangers in Their Own Land*, Arlie Russell Hochschild unravelled the 'deep story' of Tea Party supporters she met in Louisiana, paying attention to their life experiences, their disappointments and grievances, and their reasons for voting against the establishment.[21] She tells stories of people feeling unrecognised in their needs, unheard and ignored, betrayed by the established parties and their focus on corporate interests, and, thus, their deep mistrust of the democratic state they are living in. Quite similarly, Justin Gest in his book *The New Minority* has traced a sense of displacement and marginalisation among the white working class in, as he called certain towns, 'post-traumatic places'. In East London, for example, he describes the deprivation that people feel as a form of displacement 'from a valued position in the middle of the social order to its periphery'.[22] People who do not feel valued, recognised or heard, so it seems, are more likely to support parties that appeal to speak 'for them'.

In Germany, the rise of the AfD has driven numerous scholars from various disciplines to ask the questions of *who* is voting for the AfD and why – and why the AfD is more successful in Eastern Germany that it is in the West. Thus far, we know that AfD voters have mostly middle-class incomes, earning slightly higher than average incomes. They come from a variety of milieux and have been voting for a wide range of other parties before they turned to the AfD. The AfD is the party neither simply of the blue-collar worker nor of the unemployed. In Saxony the *decrease* of the unemployment rate has in fact gone hand in hand with an *increase* of AfD votes: it is not the party of the poor, the discontented and the fearful.

In Western Germany the AfD has gained more support in areas that are less densely populated; but the dynamics of population development are more significant than the level of population density: in areas with a shrinking density, the AfD is more successful. There is another correlation with the number of industrial jobs: in areas with a higher number of industrial jobs, the AfD has been more successful. Research has shown that most people who vote for the AfD do so as a protest vote – they are people dissatisfied and disappointed by political decisions, primarily in regard to refugee and migration politics. Generally speaking, the AfD electorate seems to consist of a conglomerate of situationally disappointed people (protest voters) and people politically convinced by the party programme (right-wing nationalists). The AfD fills a representation gap on the right of the Christian Democratic Union (Christlich Demokratische Union Deutschlands, CDU). In the end, the (German) academic landscape has been awash with hypotheses concerning the success of the AfD, while empirical knowledge about AfD voters and their motives is relatively sparse.[23]

Turning back to the participants in the Blue Party's anti-wolf citizens' forum in January 2019 in Lusatia, the debate on the wolf that night revealed that taking stock of the trouble brewing in our land is not simple. What is at stake, besides wolves, is the question of what actually constitutes a *demos*, that is, a people with a will that legitimises political decisions in regard to, for example, how to manage wolves or govern migration. First, 'the people' is a highly dynamic and flexible category, and it is applied in discursive practices to serve a situational function, that is of including some people while excluding others, in negotiating the question of who is part of the *demos* and who is not, of who really belongs to Saxony, Lusatia or Germany and who is an unwelcome and potentially dangerous intruder. Second, the exclusive definition of the *demos* is a necessary first step in debating the means and measures of how the people exert power. In a representative democracy, the will of the people is first and foremost expressed in the form of electing a representative who is legitimised to make decisions on behalf of the people who voted for them. In Saxon Lusatia, the rural population express their outrage because they want to decide on the politics of their land, and they want to take part in processes of decision-making – they are, in that sense, committed democrats. They start to take back control either by highly democratic means – forming citizens' initiatives (including vigilante groups) and gathering signatures for petitions – or by illegal measures: shooting wolves and dumping their bodies in the artificial lakes filling former opencast pits.

To the people taking part in the discussion that evening, democracy is in crisis; not because of the rise of a phenomenon academic observers call right-wing populism but because they feel politically unheard and ignored in their needs – in their community, in Germany and in Europe. They seem to express a sense for what the US researcher Lauren Berlant calls 'cruel optimism' that is integral to the promise of representative democracy: the promise of power for the people – a promise that more often than not remains vague and empty.[24]

If the wolf is a problem, what can a citizen in a democracy do to solve it? The first idea of the participants in the citizens' forum that evening was to petition the Saxon government. It was fruitless. The petition gathered 18,000 signatures and yet did not seem to change anything discernible, as they explain. An anti-wolf citizens' initiative has been active for years, but there seemed to be no results at all for their political struggle. On the contrary, as the dentist states, they feel insulted by the government (repeatedly marked as 'Green', which of course, it is not). At the end of the evening, Engelbert Merz explained that a referendum would be a last option. 'Just let the people vote!' When we spoke to

Merz a couple of weeks later, he explained that initiating a referendum in Saxony was a near-impossibility: 'You'll need 450,000 signatures in order to force a referendum – when Saxony has only four million inhabitants.' In the meantime, Merz had become active in a new citizens' initiative (Bürgeriniative Sachsen), with the objective of Germany leaving the EU (*Dexit*), or, if that is not possible, Saxony leaving Germany (*Säxit*). In our conversation, Merz emphasised that his political activities were characterised – in contrast to the representative system and party politics – by a grassroots democratic approach. In other words, he sees himself as a better democrat than every politician sitting in any parliament. Engelbert Merz wants problems to be solved, and he is making use of every democratic means at his disposal. 'Just let the people vote' is a phrase that Merz repeats often in our conversations.

However, regarding the wolf problem, the *demos* and its will are revealed to be not general at all but decidedly contested. Not a single *demos* exists but a fractured and multiple people: a people that wants to integrate wolves, a people that wants its population to be regulated, a people that wants wolves shot, a rural people, an urban people, a Green people, a conservationist people, a resentful people and a content people. It was unambiguous, however, during the Blue Party's anti-wolf forum in Neudorf Klösterlich that evening that representative democracy is failing in the eyes of the rural dignitaries, and they were unambiguous about whose fault that is: here, the reason for a crisis of democracy are neither the populists, the unheard, the disappointed nor the worried citizens. To the Lusatian citizens present at the inn, *you* are the crisis of democracy; 'you', that is, Green Party voters living in the comfort of the cities without wolves attacking your non-existent sheep. To them, it is incomprehensible why urban, romantic conservationists have the temerity to dump the costs of the resettlement of wild predators on to a sidelined part of the population whose opinions do not seem to matter. To them, this does not seem democratic. To them, urban, wealthy, over-educated liberals are behaving like feudal lords, not even hearing the locals if they play the game of petitions and letters.

In the discussion on the evening in Neudorf Klösterlich, a woman elaborates her complaint:

> My son had an encounter with three wolves. He was riding his bike on the way back from school with wolves running along beside him. Something like that just makes you queasy. In a situation like that, you don't take out your smartphone to take a picture, you get away as quickly as you can. We didn't report it. He says, 'What can I say? Nobody will believe me.' Some might say, be happy you saw the wolves. But he said that he was petrified. I think we need to ask: Who can discount my fear? All I hear is, 'Dear lady, you're just a wolf hater, you're too afraid, and you're just a stupid peasant.' But it's a fact: I am afraid.

She says 'they' (the Greens, the urbanites, the politicians) expect her to share their elation at the renaturing of Eastern Germany, but, unlike her, they are participating in this exciting event from behind a screen: her son is approached by a large predator as he cycles home from school. And the icing on the cake is that she is belittled and judged for her fear by people – politicians – in the distant centres of power in Dresden, in Berlin and in Brussels whose children experiences live predators behind fences in zoos and on YouTube videos.

Her fear is real. It is also used by far-right parties to legitimise politics of exclusion,[25] as became clear, for example, in the AfD politician Hilse's second address to the Bundestag in October 2019:

To talk about wolves is not just to talk about money, it is to talk about feelings. I realise that empathy for the common man cannot be expected from those who have been seated here [cries of 'Impertinence!' from the back benches], but just this once I would like you to put yourself into the shoes of a shepherd who finds several of his sheep that he has raised since birth barely alive, disembowelled and with gnawed limbs in the field in the morning; or think of the 10-year old girl who finds a sheep in her garden, directly in front of her kitchen window, covered in blood, giving her a pleading look – and missing half its hind leg. Can you imagine, this girl does not care for your statistics that say that no wolf has eaten a human in Germany. No, for she is afraid. Afraid for her life and the life of her little brothers and sisters. And this fear is not waiting for the AfD to turn up and explain the danger of the wolf. This fear comes from inside. It is innate.[26]

Some see this mobilisation of fear as a 'dangerous anti-politics'[27] and possibly even a threat to democracy.[28] But the woman whose son cycled with wolves is asking: Whose fears can be articulated as legitimate in political discourse? And whose expressions of feelings are legitimate, eligible and qualified to induce political change, and whose are discounted and remain irrelevant?

A couple of weeks after that evening, we returned to Lusatia to meet Stephan Kaasche, a volunteer at the Wolves in Saxony Contact Office (Kontaktbüro Wölfe in Sachsen), a government-funded information centre. The Contact Office works closely with the German LUPUS Institute for Wolf Monitoring and Research. He explains that the AfD is attractive to those who are feeling the loss of industrial jobs after the reorganisation of the country, which also involved a reorganisation of property rights to land and to real estate. In the GDR, every piece of real estate and every parcel of land was held in common (*Volkseigentum*). After the end of the GDR, the land was sold 'to people who had the money to buy it', explained Kaasche. And so most of the land, most of the real estate and most of the businesses in Eastern Germany do not belong to Eastern Germans. For just after reunification most Eastern Germans did not have the required financial means – no properties, no assets, no heritage and no access to credits. It was the Western Germans who 'bought' the East. This is the context in which the resentment against urban elites is festering. In 2019 – thirty years after the start of reunification – a multiplicity of asymmetries between East and West continue to exist: people have lower wages and lower pensions, feel disowned, and of top of that disenfranchised and under-represented. What Kaasche refers to as a 'sense of social injustice' is being taken up politically, and by many parties on the democratic spectrum. Petra Köpping, Minister for Integration in Saxony and a Social Democrat, wrote a book on Eastern German resentment. The provocatively titled *Integrate Us* [Eastern Germans] *First!* – that is, before the migrants and the refugees – was a best-seller in 2018.[29] Eastern German resentment is being heard, if a little late.

Only since reunification have wolves been returning, mainly populations that have come from the Baltic countries through Poland, Stephan Kaasche explains,

> because the wolves find food in abundance here and they like our post-mining landscapes. Some people are now afraid of going into the forests, but you don't need to be afraid, you can go foraging for mushrooms as before. Two hundred years ago, some wolves had rabies and bit people. But we are monitoring all the animals to check whether they're healthy. Rabies is not a problem these days. By the way, the main rabies carriers are foxes and bats. And a lot more people die of influenza than rabies.

Stephan Kaasche gives talks like these – wolf edutainment – about three times a week, in schools and nursing homes. He is a popular guest invited to all kinds of events. Essentially, his job boils down to management of fear. He can provide all the arguments why no one needs to be afraid of wolves; he is up to date on all the monitoring data; his slides contain photographs and videos of wolves from many angles; an audio recording of a howling female wolf ('looking for a partner,' he explains) seems to be the highlight of his talks. Sometimes, he feels, people seem to be ashamed to say that they are afraid of wolves.

Kaasche takes us to the fields and forests to look for wolves and their traces. We arrived at a lookout point ' overseeing a huge former open-air mining pit now filled with frozen water, a so called recultivated zone, a power station steaming on the horizon, and watched the sun set (see Figure 0.3). The wolf stayed absent, and invisible, but

Figure 0.3 Lusatia, wolf country.

the signs of its presence are hard to miss for the locals, as Kaasche explains:

> Once I was invited to a village where sheep had been killed by wolves. I wanted to talk about protection measures; the locals said, 'you can't keep animals any more'. Three sheep had been killed. In a village like that, not many, but maybe ten people, sometimes twenty; let's say everybody keeps three sheep. And when was the last kill? In some villages, there's one every year or more. But in that village, three sheep were killed – over a period of ten years. So I said: 'Think about how many sheep have been bred during the last ten years, how many have been slaughtered, how many have been eaten, and now the wolf comes once!' But that's how they tell the story: No animals can be kept any more. But that's not right, is it? And I notice that the *great fear* is that it *will* get worse. [... They're afraid] that it might repeat itself [though it happened only once]. But experience shows that it won't go on like that.

What most people see of the wolves is the carnage they can leave behind. Images of killed sheep are frequent in newspaper articles, and Facebook groups such as Wolves in Germany? No thanks! (Wölfe in Deutschland? Nein danke!) post and repost images of killed sheep from different angles, with different bones sticking out and intestines spread across fields, though from many countries and pictures collected over the course of decades. This proliferation of images of massacred ruminants – the bloodier they are, the more comments and likes a post gets – renders the wolf visible as a problem – or, as Stephan Kaasche would put it: Nobody *sees* the benefit of the wolf for the forest because it eats sick animals or because it reduces the number of deer nibbling down new forest growth. The images of sheep cadavers turn the presence of the wolf into an event, a spectacle; as we become the spectators, the wolf is transformed into a monstrous killer. This spectacular display of the wolf who is mainly present in the form of the dead sheep contributes to its suitability as an object of fear. And so it comes that there is a fusing of the ciphers of fear. This, then, is the topic of this book: as the wolf appears on the land, right-wing nationalist parties are politically taking over the depopulated, newly privatised territories in which it roams. The form in which the wolf becomes visible to most of us constitutes a distinct reality – a reality that has taken on a highly dramatic political form (see Figure 0.4).

Argument of the book

In *folk imaginaries*, wolves as a mythological figure are alluring, partly because they figure as a threat to our civilisation, and partly because one can hope to become a wolf oneself, establishing one's own order and deciding who belongs and who does not. The debates around the returning wolves amount to a politicisation of rural conflicts and a revival of the democratic spirit in rural areas, even though it goes hand in hand with a deeply populist criticism of current elites – but people in the Eastern German peripheries seem to want to decide their own fate, the policies of their territories and the governance of the *demos*. In an attempt to explain the extraordinary success of new right-wing populist parties in the Eastern German state elections in 2019, we try to understand the dissatisfactions with establishment parties, the hopes for change and what this has to do with wolves. The scope of our perspective is broad: We trace the developments of the far right in Eastern Germany since the reunification in 1989, furthering an understanding of why right-wing populist parties are gaining popularity among the rural population, and elaborate on the affective politics that their appeal is

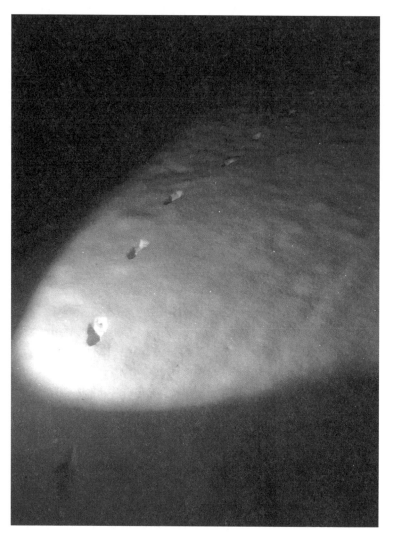

Figure 0.4 Possible trace of wolf.

based on. The argument of this book is an attempt to move beyond stereotypic representations of Eastern Germany, and shine light on the complexities of post-socialist life and losses.

Thirty years after German reunification, there are still significant differences between Eastern and Western Germany –
all socio-demographic comparisons show clearly where the
border was until thirty years ago: in terms of an ageing society, shrinking municipalities, poverty and the tendency to
vote for far-right parties. With the exception of Berlin, 'the
East' remains different in every socio-demographic respect;
it is poorer, older, more rural and more desolate than 'the
West'. People are also more likely to vote for right-wing
parties like the AfD. One might conclude that the socio-
economic data are predictors for the far-right vote, that is,
that people living in areas of high relative poverty, emigration of young people and shrinking villages and cities
are politically drawn to the far right – but this is not quite
adequate as an explanation. For the willingness to vote for
the right differs regionally – Mecklenburg for instance is
more like Bavaria than the rest of the East in terms of AfD
votes, and the AfD vote in eastern Saxony is twice as high
as in western Thuringia – so socio-demographic data are not
reliable predictors of these differences. In this book we are
trying to find an explanation for these disparities and the
logics and narratives that feed the attractiveness of the right.

In the first chapter we provide insights into the broader
context of the Eastern German experiences since the reunification in 1989. Post-reunification life in Eastern Germany
proves to be a crucial backdrop to explain why people there
feel particularly disenfranchised and why this is coming to
a head now. The transition to a united Germany was full of
broken promises of 'blooming landscapes', disappointments
and sentiments of one's own past being devalued by Western
Germans. We trace the prevailing narratives about 'the East'
that have emerged along massive structural changes. Today
the deindustrialised and depopulated landscapes not only

provide new spaces for a returning wildlife including wolves but also reveal the complete economic, political and cultural change for millions of people who may have won a peaceful revolution but lost their country in the process. We explore the popularity-gaining narrative depicting the aftermath of the peaceful revolution as an imperialist act by Western Germans who have come to take over the East to then move on to despise the locals whom they subjugated. Furthermore, we investigate the narrative that angry, 'left-behind' people are to blame for the rise of nationalism in the East, because they have been supposedly more affected by the large-scale transitions since 1989. We argue that the narratives about 'the East' we present in this chapter are not the only ones representative of people's lived and recounted reality, yet they demonstrate the contested nature of 'the East' as a narrative trope in searching for explanations for the rise of the right. Eastern Germany is not in dire straits, but many of the circulating narratives claim it to be.

People do not vote for the AfD because they are Eastern German, but the narrative of a colonised and 'left-behind' East near a demographic collapse – threatened by an 'invasion' of 'criminal foreigners' and the return of ravenous wolves alike – is being taken up by a variety of parliamentary and non-parliamentary far-right entrepreneurs who frame 'the East' as the real, genuinely German Germany. While they consider the West as 'lost' to cultural decadence and 'Islamisation', the East has become a screen of projection for the far right's visions of 'national rebirth' and as the future vantage point for 'reconquering' Germany, as we will explore in the second chapter. The rise in nationalist sentiment has manifested in an increase of racist attacks and far-right demonstrations. The summer of 2018 saw the comeback of one of the worst aspects of life in the East: the return of public affrays, pogroms and racist demonstrations that had been so common in the early 1990s just after the peaceful revolution. One of the aims of far-right splinter groups is to take over the public sphere in Eastern Germany by taking over urban spaces through highly visible 'peace marches' (against migrants), 'silent marches' (on the occasion of violence by refugees) and demonstrations commemorating 'the slaughter of Dresden' in 1945. Pogroms are not always publicly organised, however, though they are never as spontaneous as their defenders claim. They are demonstrations of power, they are intended to undermine the state's monopoly over the legitimate use of force and they serve to intimidate the left and liberal members of civil society. We show that the political standing of Saxony, and of the Eastern German states in general, remains complicated. Eastern Germany does have a past different from that of Western Germany, but a narrative of this past, how it frames the present and how it might project into the future is largely omitted from the national narratives of the Federal Republic of Germany. Events such as the 2018 Chemnitz riots and pogroms act like triggers to the struggle of which narrative we should tell about 'the East' – while for many observers these pogrom-like incidents are a validation of the 'Dark Germany' (*Dunkeldeutschland*) narrative that has been prevalent since the 1990s, for the far right these are read as symptoms of an ascendant resistance movement against an impending 'replacement' of the 'truly' German people. As we will show, these narratives unravel highly contested social realities, and each of these narratives serve political purposes.

In Chapter 3 we focus on the far right's imaginaries about 'the East' in the context of the history of *Heimat*, the politics of renaturing and the national socialist and new right-wing views on natural habitats for the German ethnos and German flora and fauna. Western Germans are recruited to move to the white enclaves in the East, as the land is cheap, institutions easy to take over and the country so unpopulated that social control is minimised. The land stands for more than just agricultural opportunities: the blood and soil logics amount to a geo-determinism, the idea that a people 'belongs to' a particular land. Unless the right people till the soil and defend their habitat, the habitat will be lost and the people will go extinct. We explain what it is like in parts of Brandenburg and Mecklenburg in 'white' villages, and hear from a hunter who explains that the AfD is not about to solve the problem of representation, but is still more attractive than any other party. The turn of nationalist (West) Germans to the East to repopulate the imagined 'empty lands' goes hand in hand with ideas of 'purification' of German territories and strong anti-immigration, anti-globalisation, anti-system and anti-cosmopolitan attitudes. As we talk to different people who were, in some way or another, affected by the wolf issue, among them farmers, hunters, local residents in rural areas and conservationists, the micro-politics that relate to the wolf problem are revealed. Wolf politics often serves as an entry point for expressing deep-felt disparagement towards urban dwellers and Western Germans. Here, the wolf represents more than just a predatory animal, but offers a metaphor for the idea that the urban population tends to patronise and belittle the rural population through habits such as hunting. Furthermore, the wolf operates as a figure with which different narratives of a German nation, a German *Volk*, and the *Heimat* are thought of, imagined, and ultimately, disputed. The figure of the wolf is a protagonist in the politics of fear that helps far-right populist parties such as the AfD appear as a party that cares for the needs and worries of the rural population, while simultaneously tapping into widespread anti-immigration, anti-urban and anti-government resentments.

The potentially violent and even murderous consequences of these narratives and the politics of 'us' against 'them' they imply have become undeniable: once again right-wing terror is on the rise in Germany. While some observers evaluate recent events as 'lone wolves terrorist attacks', others warn of a more systematic mainstreaming of far-right attitudes and their role in the increasing numbers of terrorist attacks. In Chapter 4 we discuss state and state-sponsored reactions to these political shifts, affecting policies, civil society and journalism. In particular we are looking at the governance of right-wing nationalism in a country that is widely thought of as having successfully denazified itself and come to terms with its troubled past. The fight-back by different state agents, organisations, politicians and institutions is broad and multifaceted. The goal is to influence civil society by setting a clear line between problematic ('Nazi') nationalism and acceptable, civilised, nationalism. To the well-researched theme of the governance of German nationalism, we add the East German perspective, which is not entirely aligned with the federal perspective – mainly due to a historically different understanding of the 'problematic' German nation and the second German dictatorship, which leads to greater attention to the governance of 'problematic' nationalisms. Partially in response to this, we develop a case study of the leftist Eastern German 'Anti-German' movement, which has not received much attention in academic studies in the anglophone world.

In Chapter 5, we return to the politics of fear that is central in understanding the rise of the far right and its focus on wolf politics in Eastern Germany. Against reasonable predictions that fears of widespread and humiliating underemployment, systemic poverty, terrible pensions, demographic change and empty villages, Western hegemony and Eastern subjugation, identity and history loss, even Western colonialism affect voting behaviours, we find that empirically ascertained fears focus on what are in fact negligible changes: a few new migrants here, a wolf there. This is why an analysis of the politics of fear is interesting: Affective politics use fear to mobilise, and people bask in the resonance this seems to bring. Fear, then, of either wolves or migrants, has a function, and it is this functionality of fear that we address in this chapter in order to explain, in an accessible way, the question of the rise of the right. We show what part the discussion of the wolves plays in this development, and how a politics of fear serves the aims of the AfD, not by manipulating or taking up sentiments already existing in the population but by a theatre of resistance in which 'feeling rules' (a term coined by Arlie R. Hochschild) are coming to be contested. Thus on the one hand, conditioned by imagined realities, the core of the wolf problem is a composition of fear and outrage. Objects of fear are not only the products of fantasy but an important and effective driving force in politics. The promotion and mobilisation of fear have an old tradition in German politics, as the term 'German angst' illustrates. On the other hand, the current discourses of fear are functional for the populist agents who disseminate them: for them, they justify insurrection and racism, and they legitimate the breaking of the boundaries of civility.

The final chapter summarises the argument of the book and provides answers to our guiding questions: What does the trope of the wolf tell us about the state of democracy in Eastern Germany? Why is anti-establishmentarianism prevalent in rural areas? And why does it seem to be more prevalent in Eastern Germany? And ultimately, how can we understand the re-emergence and strengthening of national-ist and xenophobic attitudes and political actors in Eastern German in more depth?

1

The 'East':
Depopulation, deindustrialisation,
colonialism

We are seeing demographic change to the extent that not
only is Germany coming to be the oldest country in Europe,
but Saxony is the oldest region of Germany. And this is
particularly significant in peripheral, ageing areas that are
left behind. And so the periphery is revolting against being
ignored. To summarise, the young are gone, the wolves are
coming back.[1]

Frank Richter, civil rights activist in the 1989
peaceful revolution, author and politician

The Eastern Germans won a revolution,
but lost their country

The right-wing populist political party Alternative für
Deutschland (AfD, Alternative for Germany) has been
increasingly successful in elections all across Germany, and
in particular across Eastern Germany, where it has been
the second strongest party in the recent regional elections
in all of the Eastern German states or *Länder*. Why this is
has been a puzzle. Voters for the AfD were long deemed to
be poor, male and elderly, but either this has changed or
further research has proved it to be wrong. It appears that
people who vote for nationalist parties have one thing in

common: They are unhappy with the way things are.[2] But many would argue that the status quo in Eastern Germany is better than the socialist dictatorship that had caused unprecedented environmental degradation, and since 1990 billions of Deutsche Mark and later Euros have been poured and continue to be poured into building up the infrastructure, paying for social services and rebuilding a thoroughly run-down country. Do the inhabitants of this region and the recipients of so much generosity even have the right to be unhappy? Or are they, as some argue, victims of a vicious colonialism by self-satisfied prigs, bringing baubles while plundering the country of its assets and dividing up all the good jobs amongst themselves? What, in other words, is going on in Eastern Germany to explain the extent of unhappiness that scholars identify to be the main reason to vote for the AfD?

The Wolves Are Coming Back is one answer to that question for the following reasons. First, the environment in Eastern Germany had been devastated by heavy industry and coal mining operations. The federal government of the reunited Germany closed down most of these sources of pollution, and in the course of the last thirty years has reversed a great deal of the environmental degradation: there is just much more nature for wolves to come back to. Second, the wall came down. That is, the wall between the Germanys in 1989, but also the border between Germany and Poland in 2004. Wolves swam across the rivers that border the countries, roamed westwards and found the sort of loosely forested landscapes they were used to in the eastern Baltics and Poland. Third, *de*population has rapidly accelerated since the end of the GDR. Cities, towns and villages have been shrinking. In particular, medium-sized and large towns have lost a considerable segment of their population since the 1990s. Hoyerswerda, for instance, in the 1980s a city of seventy thousand inhabitants, has lost 60 per cent of its population since 1990 and is continuing to shrink. And with every lost citizen, there is less local demand, more closed shops, fewer jobs in retail, lower business tax revenues, a poorer municipality, greater difficulties in maintaining local infrastructure, fewer jobs in infrastructure and more reasons to leave: contracting towns are caught in a cycle of shrinkage. But shrinking towns leave more unpopulated lands, where deer and boars can roam and wolves roam right behind.

Thus, even though the twenty-first century is a century of urbanisation, the urban centres of most East German towns (Chemnitz, Halle, Magdeburg and Rostock and thus most towns except for the biggest ones, Leipzig, Dresden and Jena) have lost roughly 20 per cent of their populations. Even the most successful Eastern German cities, Dresden and Leipzig, have achieved their slight population gains since the 1990s mainly through incorporation of other local authorities under the guise of administrative consolidation. And whilst Germany overall has doubled its population since the 1900s, the Eastern states have just about maintained their population sizes since then. Populations of the Eastern states have been decreasing since the founding of the GDR and have been continuing to decrease at a slightly higher pace since the 1990s.[3] The rural areas are seeing this decrease at a particularly fast pace; some areas have reached the population levels of the mid-nineteenth century.

The shrinking of the population has allowed for renaturing to take place, hence the steady increase of wolves. Concurrently, visible signs of far-right youth culture and populist sentiments have been increasing, too. It seems that we have witnessed not only a rewilding of the Eastern German environment but a rewilding of Eastern German politics, too. The return of nationalist populism has been a particularly visible change in Eastern Germany, manifesting in the increasing success of the AfD and the persistence of weekly PEGIDA rallies in Dresden since 2014. Among the manifold narratives and explanations being contemplated in journalistic, academic and political debates around the question of why people in Eastern Germany seem more susceptible to the return of populist nationalism, one claim has been particularly predominant: Eastern Germans were said to be (wrongly) angry while having nothing to be angry about. Within the thirty years of post-reunification, Eastern Germans have been continuously classified as second-hand citizens, as backward and full of resentments. This dominant narrative about 'the East' has been coined and frequently repeated by West German scholars, journalists and politicians – it is a narrative about people who are *not quite German*, but rather seen as a minority bewildered by new cultural codes, routines, action orientations, expectations, assessments and an entire institutional order that was imported wholesale from another country that had spent forty years developing it.[4]

The Western German sociologist Helmuth Berking explained that the stability of the GDR seems to have been an effect of the intertwined political forces of assimilation and reward, combined with an apparatus of coercion, the Ministry for State Security (Ministerium für Staatssicherheit, MfS), commonly known as the Stasi.[5] Berking thus shows GDR inhabitants to be a people of victims and conformists: publicly compliant, privately dissident. Because the type of socialism developed in the GDR allocated and distributed resources not in reliable, rules-based, administrative relationships but in an unmediated manner, making social and public life person-based and proximate.[6] With the transformation, 'communities bound by years of common economic shortages' floundered.[7] The land formerly held in common was re-privatised. Many people became unemployed. Berking argues that all experienced being pushed into an inferior position and being robbed of their own biographies, having their political and cultural elites excluded, witnessing a hitherto inconceivable level of social disintegration and sharing both a new resentment against the West and the feeling of being losers.

Furthermore, he argues that the political system of the GDR was based mainly on external constraints, whilst Western German society combined external with internal self-constraints.[8] The official and the informal rules of the new institutions were thus often experienced as bewildering, complex and unspoken, with people made to feel incompetent, subject to 'coerced self-invalidation and institutionally prescribed inferiority',[9] as those who did know the rules came to impose them. Thus, Western German managers, teachers, administrators and professors came to the East in the 1990s to help establish their old order as a new order in the Eastern states. A generation later, they still divide the most powerful, most well-paid and most visible positions amongst themselves. Berking explains that

> 40 years of cultural modernization in the West – slotted under the laudatory keywords: Individualization, detraditionalization and pluralization of lifeforms – have generated a West German social character and a symbolic order which coldly gazes, with a complete lack of understanding, upon those whose personal identities, socialization, and sociation were formed by years of life in a bygone socialism depicted as inferior in absolutely *every* way.[10]

According to this narrative, besides having to submit to new rules, social expectations and career paths, East Germans found their cultural, political, media and academic elites almost entirely replaced by Western Germans. In fact, Western Germans basically ran the country after 1989, in all parts of Germany, and mostly continue to do so. Even the AfD, a party whose voters live predominantly in the East, is run by Western Germans.[11] In this, the AfD does not differ from most of the other parties. There are several probable reasons for this. First, Eastern Germans are much less likely to be actively involved in political party organising, and so there are just fewer candidates to run for office; this is exacerbated by the significant brain drain to the West, and a brain gain from the West. Second, it might be a feature of Eastern German culture, affecting the likelihood of their applying for powerful and highly visible positions, being more risk-averse, having less self-efficacy. The third reason given is that the positions of power were handed to Western Germany thirty years ago, and they just prefer 'their own kind', excluding minorities of various kinds from positions of influence and marginalising Eastern Germans as a quasi-ethnicity.[12] So the AfD is in no way special in this regard.

After reunification, many found themselves relegated to a superfluous class; manufacturing bases closed, service sectors were relegated to the West, teachers, administrators and engineers replaced by Western German personnel. The German Council of Economic Experts had foreseen these developments in 1991, before the East German currency was abolished:

> Consumers obtaining the West German Mark and thus a convertible currency will want to buy West German consumer goods. The East German economy will lose spending capacity. The East German companies will see themselves

helplessly at the mercy of international competition. The revenues will plummet [...] Salaries and employment levels will also plummet. The short-term advantage in gaining access to West German consumer goods by introducing the West German mark in the GDR will be followed by a rebound, as the East Germans will ultimately destroy their own revenue base.[13]

These predictions tragically came to pass. The voters had been led to expect flourishing landscapes by the reigning Western German chancellor Helmut Kohl. Kohl knew better, but also he knew how to win elections. He later admitted that he knew at the time that the introduction of the West Germany currency would devastate the country, and so the flourishing landscapes were a downright lie: 'We deliberately played down the rotten state of the economy – that was no accidental omission, we had discussed this – we knew, or thought we knew that this was the right thing to do from a psychological perspective.'[14] And Kohl won the first general German elections by a landslide.

Exchanging Eastern German marks for Western German marks (*Deutsche Mark*, DM) was enticing at first glance. Finally, Western goods would be available to everyone, when they had been a privilege for the well-connected. And Western German welfare benefits amounted to about DM 800 a month for a family. The Eastern German retirement pension meanwhile amounted to 380 Eastern German Marks. With the currency exchange came the Western German welfare state, and much higher average incomes: even on welfare people would earn considerably more than on their usual wages. The usual exchange rate of seven-to-one for the Eastern German mark meant that Western German welfare payments came to five times the average monthly wage. Given the onset of a mass exodus towards the West, an exchange rate of one-to-one was promised in the hope of stalling mass migration from the East, and this was initially a boon to Eastern Germans, at least for those with savings. It was also poison for the Eastern German economy. The exchange rate in effect quadrupled the price of Eastern German goods, making them unattractive to their previous market in Eastern Europe. Tragically, as the vice president of the Eastern German state bank, Edgar Most, put it, the Eastern Germans democratically chose to commit economic suicide.[15]

To explain how this devastated the country, a few details on the GDR economy are necessary. By 1989 the GDR had had 8.6 million employees, yet three years later only 6.2 million remained – almost a third had disappeared from the statistics.[16] Virtually an entire generation – everyone over fifty-five – was made to retire *en bloc*.[17] More than a hundred thousand foreign contract workers were made redundant. The first to go were the employees of the secret services and other regime-specific white-collar workers. Half a year later, massive unemployment also hit skilled workers and unskilled labourers, and women especially lost their jobs in large numbers. Of all employed workers in the GDR, half had been blue-collar workers. In Eastern Germany these now make up fewer than a quarter of all employees. The Eastern German proletarians quickly moved from being the dominant class to being a small minority, without rosy prospects for the future.[18] Many found themselves in the decade after reunification in often pointless retraining programmes, working short-time or placed in work-creation schemes – many of which kept the unemployment statistics looking better than they in fact were. Those who found work were paid at a very low rate. What happens globally to the working classes happened at lightning speed in

Eastern Germany: as the historian Ilko-Sascha Kowalczuk has argued, it has thus unwittingly become a laboratory of globalisation, particularly with regards to its most unpleasant aspects.[19]

In retrospect, though, those who bemoan the demise of their country don't focus on the monetary economy but focus their blame on the main institutional agent of this change. This was was an organisation that had originally been founded to modernise ramshackle GDR industries. It was called Trust Agency (Treuhand) and had been installed by the last GDR government. It was responsible for 12,000 companies, of which 1,588 were returned to previous owners, 310 were handed over to municipalities and 6,546 were privatised. About 30 per cent of the companies were liquidated.[20] All in all, 2.6 million jobs were lost. Yet the taxpayer spent 166 billion DM on this modernisation programme and received only 39.9 billion DM in sales: everyone, it seems, lost out. Eastern Germans lost incomes, jobs, dignity, real estate and their country, and the Western Germans lost a huge amount of money as well as the goodwill of the new citizens.[21] The Treuhand thus has come to stand for predatory capitalism, Western German colonialism and the uncoordinated selling of Eastern German national wealth for Western German benefit, and is blamed for everything that has gone wrong since unification. In the West the institution is largely ignored. Yet the Treuhand changed all structures of ownership, from the restitution of nationalised land, forests and palaces to the factory owners, landowners and estate owners who had moved West during communism. But consumer behaviour was also partly to blame. As soon as the Eastern German Mark was exchanged one-to-one for the Western German DM, people wanted to buy Western goods with their Western money. Freedom fighters turned into economic migrants in a flash, as a Western German journalist derisively put it recently.[22]

The Western German claim that Eastern Germans have no right no be angry and should inherently be grateful, because the inhabitants of the former GDR only profited from the reunification in 1989, turns out to be problematic. This popular narrative conceals the drastic realities of post-unification life in Eastern Germany and dismisses the complicity of Western German politics in the economic devastation that affected the East particularly in the 1990s. The Eastern Germans may have won a revolution peacefully, but they lost a country in the process.

Western German colonialism: 'This house used to stand in another country'

In the Brunnenstrasse in Berlin, a residential house has been painted with a slogan 'This house used to stand in another country', and in smaller lettering above, 'Human volition can shift everything' (see Figure 1.1). This slogan reflects the sentiment of many older Eastern Germans who argue that they feel like strangers in their own land.[23] The disenchantment with the political, demographic and economic change is mirrored in the reframing of the social environment in which people live. Cities have been renamed from Karl-Marx-Stadt to Chemnitz, and street names changed from Rosa-Luxemburg to John F. Kennedy. As the urban sociologist Mary Dellenbaugh-Losse argued in her dissertation, 'signs of the former regime were cleared away to make way for capitalism, democracy, and the free market', and these changes 'took many forms, from street names to urban planning'.[24] People in the East might not have changed, but their environment, including the people around them, did.

Figure 1.1 'This house used to stand in another country.' Idea and execution by Jean-Remy von Matt, in the Brunnenstraße, Berlin.

The economic devastation of the East, the symbolic restructuring of public places, and the imposition of new ways of being has been reframed as colonialism.[25] The hypothesis of colonialism has been taken up by a new generation of Eastern German journalists and publicists such as Jana Hensel and Martin Machowecz who problematise the East's alleged economic exploitation by the West. In an interview with the *Berliner Zeitung* in 2017, the head of the Federal Agency for Civic Education (Bundeszentrale für politische Bildung), Thomas Krüger, stated that, almost three decades after the reunification, the lack of indigenous Eastern German elites is being 'experienced as a cultural colonialism'.[26] Even in academic discourses, the colonialist narrative has made some incursions. Fran den Hertog hypothesises a German-German colonial history.[27] Not only did the population have to suffer from the economic restrutcturing[28] and the wholesale exchange of elites since 1990,[29] the public discourse about Eastern Germany has also been dominated by Western Germans.[30] The experiences of Eastern Germans, as Daniel Kubiak and Naika Foroutan have argued, are comparable with those of 'people with a migration background': both migrants and Eastern Germans share experiences of social inequality and political alienation and are further 'affected by social, cultural and identificative devaluation'.[31] Elsewhere we have shown how 'the Ossi' ('the Eastie') has been produced as a discourse figure with 'unwanted migration experience'.[32]

Against this background of researching 'the' Eastern Germans,[33] and thirty years after the transformation, two very successful and widely read books have taken up the grief of the East. In 2018 the Saxon Minister for Integration, Petra Köpping, published a book with the provocative title *Integrate Us First! (Integriert doch erst mal uns!)*, whilst the theologian and civil rights activist in the 1989 peaceful revolution Frank Richter published *Does Saxony Still Belong to Germany? (Gehört Sachsen noch zu Deutschland?)* in 2019. Both can be read as attempts to offer new ways of narrating and seeing the East.

Petra Köpping argues that economic, cultural and structural aspects prove a colonialist situation. She argues that, first, a third of the population in the East earns less than €10 per hour, living on the poverty line. Second, the East has fewer company pensions, much lower levels of inheritance, and lower real-estate assets – all of these factors contribute to the people being considerably poorer and transmitting that poverty to the next generation.[34] Third, Eastern Germans continue to appear less distinguished in their public self-presentations, partly because they are less likely to come from the old bourgeoisie. All this because of the Treuhand, Köpping argues, which organised an immense asset transfer from East to West:[35] a scam by West German capitalists against the East German proletariat who had been so hopeful at unification. So they were scammed out of their lifetime achievements.[36]

In Frank Richter's narrative, the year 1989 was not as such exploitative, it was rather a reset for Germany and the Germans, and a peaceful achievement at that: the Germans – of all people! – succeeded in a revolution at the end of that century, a revolution characterised by the slogan 'no violence!'[37] However, he argues, tragically the Eastern Germans voted *Anschluss*.[38] As with the previous *Anschluss* of Austria to national socialist Germany in 1938, Richter implies that, although the population democratically and willingly submitted to a 'foreign power', this unwittingly resulted in an occupation of the land by (Western) Germans, basically allowing for a hostile takeover. Richter also sees the Treuhand as the main agent of this hostile takeover.[39] The Treuhand is thus considered by many the gravedigger of the GDR. Horst Köhler, controller of the Treuhand and later German President, is widely quoted in the East as having said on 23 January 1991, 'deaths are inevitable'.

What he meant was that death precedes resurrection.[40] But this is not how it was understood. Eastern German lives, dignity and achievements were relegated to second-class, and perhaps even dispensable.

These political treatises called for a new pride in the East and provoked responses such as Norbert Pötzl's *The Treuhand Complex* (in German, *Der Treuhand-Komplex*). Pötzl argues that the deindustrialisation of the GDR had begun far earlier than 1989. The GDR government had itself driven well-known companies out, including Siemens, Osram, Audi, Wella and Zeiss, with their anti-capitalist, anti-bourgeois policies.[41] And because the GDR government was wary of a repetition of the insurrectionist riots of 1957, it capped prices for rents, staple foods, public transport and services at prewar levels,[42] meaning that there was far too little money to invest in the modernisation of infrastructure, housing and heavy industries: by the 1980s, a quarter of factory units were over twenty years old and, by Western standards, worthless scrap metal. There was, in other words, nothing to defraud the Eastern Germans of. All they had was scrap metal, environmental degradation and urban dilapidation. The industry in Eastern Germany on the brink of reunification was so unsustainable, Pötzl argues, that even those products lauded as world-class were years behind international standards and produced at great expense. For instance, archival records show that the 256-KB chip sold in the GDR for 16 Eastern German Marks actually cost 536 Marks to produce – but on the free market, such a chip could be bought elsewhere for US$2.[43] In Pötzl's view, even the post-reunification trauma of unemployment is vastly exaggerated, statistically and in terms of the actual suffering: he argues that it was just because the Eastern Germans had had their intrinsic initiative bred out of them by the

GDR's 'right to work' scheme that they found themselves helpless after 1989.

The fault, argues this West German journalist, lies not with the impositions of capitalism but with the premodern, authoritarian and passive people the GDR government had fostered. Pötzl might get his facts right, but his interpretation does of course not disperse Eastern German resentment: the narratives on Western colonialism and Eastern suffering have taken on lives of their own. In 2019 the wolves are back, and people – for good or bad reasons – feel colonised (see Figure 1.2). This provokes some derision in the West from those who like to point out the hundreds of billions of Marks and later Euros transferred to the East of the country. They also continue to refer to Eastern Germans as somewhat less refined, a little backward, perhaps also as authoritarian, all features of Eastern German themselves that serve to explain the move of the Eastern German voter to the far right. This of course adds insult to injury.

Easterners are called victims of reunification, Eastern underdogs, and are accused of feeling nostalgia for the GDR. Their country is remembered in public discourse as a country of ubiquitous surveillance coupled with outrageous environmental pollution. But the drubbing of the Stasi turned into a defeat of everyone. The loss of the government was not the liberating adventure it has been celebrated as in the Federal Republic; for the locals, emancipation meant a wide-scale loss of jobs, and jobs were not *just* jobs. As Norbert Pötzl explained, the attempt to turn the Eastern economy into a market economy meant privatisation, and privatisation meant a good hard look at the details of companies. Pötzl used the nationally owned enterprise Automobilwerke Eisenach in Thuringia as an example. Of the 9,500 staff, merely 2,469 were employed in manufacturing cars. The

Figure 1.2 Graffiti of wolves 'We are coming' in Berlin.

others were employed in the enterprise's kindergarten, its out-patient medical clinic, its holiday accommodation, its construction division and in other appended operations.[44] When the enterprise was consolidated, it was the (largely outmoded) automobile sector that remained, while the other three-quarters of the staff were made redundant. But to lose a position in this sort of network economy is to lose the kindergarten for the children, the clinic, the sports grounds, arts and leisure centre, and the right to make use of the associated vacation homes. So unlike in the West, a job loss also meant a lost network of resilience, friendship, camaraderie, infrastructure, services, and private life, but also of rights, expectations and everyday structures. The Western taxpayer paid for the modernisation, the environmental clean-up, the social benefits, pensions, public sector workers, for seventeen million Eastern Germans who had not themselves paid into the pension plans, health insurance and social security provision. So the West incurred great costs and in exchange expected integration of grateful Eastern Germans – who saw themselves as devalued and expendable. Although many profited of course from the pension, infrastructure and social security plans, they remained the poor cousins from whom gratitude is expected. It is perhaps no wonder, then, that some Eastern Germans themselves react by reinvigorating ethno-nationalist logics whereby it is not them who are backward but other nations, other cultures, other religions.[45]

Today, the East is still visible on maps, for instance on maps of income distribution across Germany. Thirty years after unification, average incomes in the East are nearly 20 per cent lower than in the West, the gross domestic product is 73.2 per cent of what it is in the West and, of the five hundred largest German corporations, only thirty-six have their corporate headquarters in the East, which in turn means that tax revenues are low and there are lower funds for research and development.[46] Thirty years after the reunification, the Eastern Germans remain poorer and angrier, and some of them are now turning to nationalist parties. The advantage of nationalism is that it promises a high collective status even for people who are seemingly left behind, for people who have not fulfilled their ambitions and feel cheated of their true status, as Arlie R. Hochschild and Katherine J. Cramer have shown in their studies about the 'left behind' populations in the US states of Wisconsin and Louisiana, and their reasons why they turned to nationalist and far-right parties.[47]

A country without women

In the economic turmoils of the early 1990s working-class women were made redundant first and in greater numbers, and, not wanting to live off others, they moved to the West earlier than the men, or at least they moved to the urban centres. According to the sociologist Steffen Mau, women migrated to the West because of their self-conception as economically independent and emancipated, and, as such, women succeeded in blending into the Western German labour market comparatively well.[48] According to Mau, between 1992 and 1996 the number of women migrating from the East to the West was twice as high as the number of men, and of the thirty-years-olds who left Eastern Germany between 1991 and 2005 two-thirds were women.[49] This transformation left a 'fractured society' behind, and, in particular, a 'demographic masculinisation' among the affected age groups.[50] And it is noticeable that men predominate in nationalist public affrays, demonstrations and protests such as PEGIDA. One anonymous email reached us whose author tries to explain why he is attracted to far-right movements: 'I see migrants as rivals in a cut-throat competition for the scanty jobs, the damned few women and the ever-worsening housing crisis. [...] Multinational corporations, women and landlords have an ever-greater number of people to play off one another. So this is where my hate comes from, this is why I go to the PEGIDA demonstrations.'

Angry white men certainly dominate the public displays of anger. On the basis of his research among those 'angry men' in the United States of America, Michael Kimmel identified an increase of rage among men due to the political, social and economic transformations in the US that seemed to have affected men more than women, leaving them feeling left behind, betrayed by the government and enraged about former privileges being taken away from them.[51] Similarly, the sociologist Donna Zuckerberg argues that the male members of US online far-right communities believe that 'the rise of feminism and progressivism is both the cause of the problems plaguing men and, through the "cultural narrative" they generate, the reason those problems are not taken seriously'.[52] Similarly, many blame angry white men for the rise of nationalism in Germany. 'Eastern Germany on the brink of demographic collapse' was a headline of an article in the *Financial Times* in June 2019, in which the demographic transformations in Eastern Germany were problematised as one of the contributing factors to the rise of far-right populism in these regions.[53]

Stefan Locke, the correspondent for Eastern Germany for the *Frankfurter Allgemeine Zeitung*, explained to us in an interview: 'One of the young men [joining PEGIDA] told me: "I will go to these meetings for as long as it takes me to find a woman or a job."'[54] Petra Köpping, the Minister for Integration in Saxony, quoted a man who had written her a letter in which he stated, 'Ms Köpping, if you supply me with a woman, I will stop going to PEGIDA.'[55] The problem, for many of our interview partners, seems to be men.

The Chemnitz riots in 2018 and all the far-right demonstrations such as the weekly demonstrations by PEGIDA since 2015 were dominated by men. Quite apart from the ludicrousness of expecting governments to supply people with women, what we hear from this is a warning: right-wing organisations and networks are attractive to those who feel they have nothing to lose. There is thus a strategic aspect to joining far-right and nationalist groups. As Stefan Locke puts it, 'The people leave, and the wolves are back':

> After the wall came down, [...] so many people became unemployed, tens of thousands, practically overnight. If you go to Eastern Saxony today, right at the border to Poland and the Czech Republic, you'll find a lot of abandoned houses, inner city centres which are empty, and only older people on the streets, because most of the young people left. We lost two generations actually here in the last twenty years.[56]

A narrative of depopulation and 'empty villages' without any women left to reproduce becomes prone to being exploited by far-right politics and filled with anxieties about the future. As the German expert on gerontology and rural sociology Kai Brauer argued, mobilising fear regarding the future of an ageing, rural population does produce a particular social reality. He argued that, in particular, the 'return of the wolves' narrative stands for the legitimate fear of depopulation, presenting the rural, ageing population as passive, defenceless and highly vulnerable, passively exposed to the unstoppable process of the demographic collapse.[57] But we would argue that a narrative that focuses on men as the source for the rise of the right disregards women both as active agents in the rising right and as voters for far-right parties. If the far right is imagined as ruled by toxic masculinity, the fact that women have historically been and are currently an important part of far-right movements is being obscured. Furthermore, whilst the gender politics of the far right has become a focus of scholarly attention,[58] the role of women within racist activism is highly under-researched – with the notable exception of Kathleen Blee's work in the United States.[59] According to Blee, the lack of scholarly attention to this topic makes it 'difficult to explain the adherence of substantial numbers of women to organized racism today'.[60]

Women actually play key roles as highly visible and top-ranking politicians, for instance Alice Weidel and Frauke Petry (until 2017) for the German AfD. A recent addition to the AfD regional party in Berlin is Carolin Matthie, a young woman who is also the spokesperson of the German Rifle Association, an influencer on Instagram and YouTube. She posts photos of herself carrying guns under the hashtags #girlsandguns and #womeninpower. In the far-right newspaper *Deutschland-Kurier*, she published an article titled 'How women can protect themselves against migrant violence'. She argues that training in self-defence or martial arts takes years, and that it is more effective to just carry an (alarm) gun or pepper spray – 'making it possible especially for women to make up for their physical deficits, e.g. their lower height, strength and weight, and defend themselves against physically superior attackers'.[61]

Official statistics on crime rates show their constant and steady decline spanning several decades. Still, gun sales in Germany have been increasing, particularly since the influx of refugees in the years 2015–16. What far-right influencers such as Carolin Matthie are communicating is that women *should clearly* be afraid. Matthie also makes it clear of *whom* women should be afraid. The threat they are co-construing is not diffuse but contained within the body of the 'criminal foreigner'. Sentiments of fear and insecurity can provide a space for affective engagement,[62] and far-right parties such as the AfD or racist activists' groups are eager to tap into those sentiments, to provide narratives to make sense of these sentiments, and appeal to people and finally mobilise them. In Germany the dominant narrative of far-right parties and organisations is the 'great replacement' conspiracy theory. As the story goes, the German people are being replaced by Muslim people. This replacement is allegedly planned and executed by chancellor Angela Merkel. Conspiracy theories are powerful narratives to back up campaigns of fear, because they constitute a *structure of feeling* that not only 'generates as well as registers the contradictions of contemporary social transformations'[63] but produce a particular version of reality.

All in all, while far-right parties and organisations in Germany are predominantly male, their conspiracy narratives are targeted at 'fearful women' and their male saviours. And perhaps this explains why the gender gap is narrowing: recent studies suggest that AfD voters include an ever increasing share of women. Currently, among voters in Eastern Germany, the AfD is supported by 57 per cent of men and 43 per cent of women.[64] And the main motivation is opposition to immigration.[65]

In our research we found that women are successfully mobilised by the predominant far-right narratives, and in particular their campaigns of fear, and our research suggests that these narratives tend to resonate with women in regions that have particularly suffered from the post-1989 processes of deindustrialisation and depopulation. We have looked at Suhl in southern Thuringia as an example, a small town that today is the town with the highest average population age in Germany (see Figure 1.3). Suhl has lost its major industries and has suffered from high rates of

Figure 1.3 The city of Suhl in Thuringia.

unemployment. But today the lack of jobs has been replaced by a lack of workers: Economically, Suhl has recovered with the help of many small- and medium-sized businesses. Still, the town remains depopulated, leading to many buildings standing empty, which from a governmental perspective seemed very convenient during the 2015–16 mass refugee influx, when no one knew how to provide shelter for over a million immigrants. So in 2016 the first central reception facility for refugees in Thuringia was established in Suhl. A sleepy little ageing town with too many empty buildings thus saw itself hosting thousands of people from overseas.

In November 2018 we met with Ines Graf*, a 50-year-old woman who remains active in the regional mining association. Suhl had had open-pit mines for coal, iron and salt, and Graf's regional mining association attempts to commemorate and celebrate the traditions of the old and long-gone mining culture. In our first conversation Ines Graf told us that 'Where I live now, I don't feel at home. I'm a native Thuringian. I'm the *Ossi* [the 'Eastie', a colloquial term for East Germans]. I don't feel as if I were an "All-German" (*Gesamtdeutsche*)'.[66] We asked her why she did not feel German, and she referred to the wages being different in the East, but also to the fact that some regions no longer felt familiar, with 'the foreigners' taking over entire towns. These she clearly sees as a danger to women. Our conversation with Ines Graf took place in the Waldfrieden restaurant, which is located in the low mountains surrounding Suhl, just one bus stop away from the first reception facility for refugees. We met at night for dinner, and it was a cold, stormy November evening. Outside, the wind was rustling through the trees, and, as an employee in the Suhl zoo had told us earlier that day, a wolf-dog hybrid was recently shot in the forests surrounding Suhl – the first of its kind in decades. Inside the cosy restaurant we asked Ines Graf about her thoughts about Germany's future, and she said with a grim face:

In Gera [Graf's place of birth], it's really bad. Pensioners don't dare to walk the streets any more. They plan their doctor's appointments to take place in the morning, because in the afternoon … There was this one case, a woman took the bus and a foreigner blocked the exit with his backpack and wouldn't let her exit the bus. So she put the backpack to the side and he almost tackled her – just because she touched his backpack. They are all accommodated in an old hospital, and from there, they walk into town. In the arcades, in the city centre, they're sitting around, only foreigners. No chance that a German can go and sit there. In Suhl, it isn't that bad yet, I think. But I don't know what's going to happen. In any case, there is one thing we shouldn't do: to let it get us down. But it has been glorified: 'Come to Germany. Here, you'll get money. You'll get an apartment.' Instead, these young people should just stay down there and fight for their own country.[67]

The stories of 'the foreigners' taking over entire Eastern cities were reproduced in many of our conversations with different people in different regions in the East, regardless of whether our interview partners were men or women. The fear of 'imported violence against women' is also the core of current campaigns of fear of the far right in Germany. Far-right agents such as AfD members reproduce that feeling on social media. But also mainstream media scandalise 'migrant criminality', though statistics show that migrant crime is the same level as local crime amongst similar age cohorts.

However, whilst some of the people we talked to in Saxony, Berlin and Thuringia expressed their feelings about being Eastern German in a negative way, most people did not, and the narratives about Eastern Germany that we have presented in this chapter are not the only ones representative of people's lived and recounted reality – this only demonstrates the contested nature of 'the East' as a narrative trope in searching for explanations for the rise of the right. The expert on the German far right Matthias Quent emphasised that 'Nobody will inevitably become an AfD voter due to the history of the East – in reality only a few will'.[68] People might not like the reunited Germany, but most are doing quite well in it. Unemployment is low, as are living expenses, immigration is something mainly known from the news and social networks, and, overall, life is good. But – and this seems crucial in explaining dissatisfaction – it might get bad in the future. Not because of climate change or impending war, but because of the fear over 'The Great Transformation'.[69]

Eastern Germany is thus not in dire straits, but many of the circulating narratives about the East claim it to be. People do not vote for the AfD because they are Eastern German, but the narrative of a colonised and 'left-behind' East near a demographic collapse – threatened by an 'invasion' of 'criminal foreigners' and the return of the wolves alike – is being taken up by a variety of parliamentary and non-parliamentary far-right entrepreneurs who frame the East as the real, genuinely German Germany. Whilst they consider the West as 'lost' to cultural decadence and 'Islamisation', the East has become a screen of projection for the far right's visions of 'national rebirth' and as the future vantage point for 're-conquering' Germany, as we will explore in the following chapter.

2

Wolf packs:
Pogroms, pillories and riots[1]

Today, dear friends, the question is no longer hammer or
anvil. The question today is sheep or wolf. And I – no, we –
decide under these circumstances to be wolf!

AfD politician Björn Höcke in the 4th Kyffhäuser
meeting of the AfD's *völkisch* wing,
Schloss Burgscheidungen, Saxony-
Anhalt, 23 June 2018

A short history of pogroms:
Hoyerswerda, Chemnitz and Colditz

A homicide led to a significant right-wing riot in Chemnitz
in August 2018. After an altercation at a summer festival in
the city centre, a local man was knifed and died in the early
hours of Sunday 26 August 2018. A few hours later, riots
began, involving what eyewitnesses reported as protesters
hunting down and attacking people of colour, whom they
marked as 'non-Germans' or 'refugees'. We know now that
local hooligans and members of the far-right group Kaotic
Chemnitz had called for a nationwide protest march against
Angela Merkel's refugee politics. An estimated eight hundred people followed the call under the guise of a march
of grief.[2] In the aftermath, anti-Semitic statements were

58

registered, Nazi salutes made and about twenty people injured. A video documenting these attacks referred to as *hounding* subsequently ignited considerable public controversy throughout the German media, with some politicians defending the racist attacks in public as an appropriate reaction to the homicide and to Merkel's refugee politics. The AfD MP Markus Frohnmaier for example tweeted, 'When the state cannot protect its citizens, people take to the streets to protect themselves. It's as easy as that! It is our civic duty today to stop the deadly "knife migration". It could have been your father, your son, your brother!'[3] Knife migration (*Messermigration*) is a term often used by AfD politicians to insinuate that all Germans are in perpetual danger from male migrants from Muslim countries. Incidents such as the Chemnitz homicide are then read not as individual attacks in an interpersonal altercation between young men but as evidence of a systemic problem, that is, migration from Islamic countries leaving us all unsafe and in particular, violating the uniquely European enlightened sexual order. On the next day, Monday, five thousand people gathered at a rally organised by Pro Chemnitz – a far-right initiative and voters' association[4] – in front of the Chemnitz's 13-metre Karl Marx Monument. They chanted slogans: 'We are the people' (*Wir sind das Volk*), 'Foreigners out!' and 'The national resistance prevails!'[5] The police, outnumbered and badly prepared, were not successful in separating the far-right demonstration from the counter-demonstrators. The following Saturday, thousands of people again marched through the streets in what they termed a 'silent march' – organised by AfD and PEGIDA in close co-operation with known neo-Nazi cadres. The Chemnitz racist riots demonstrated first the potential for uniting various and heterogeneous agents of the German far right,[6] and second the normalisation of expressing far-right beliefs in public without fearing social sanctioning.[7]

The month after the murder was marked by weekly demonstrations of far-right groups. Every Friday Pro Chemnitz called on its followers to march through the city's streets. They were joined by members of the far-right populist party AfD, the National Socialist parties The Third Path (*Der III. Weg*) and the National Democratic Party of Germany (Nationaldemokratische Partei Deutschlands, NPD), the NPD's youth organisation Young Nationalists (Junge Nationalisten) and the neo-nationalist party The Right (Die Rechte). Also, a kaleidoscope of other formal and informal far-right groups followed the call, among them hooligan organisations such as Kaotic Chemnitz, anti-migration groups such as Future Homeland (Zukunft Heimat), martial arts clubs such as Imperium Fight Team, racist activist groups such as the Identitarian Movement, neo-Nazi groups such as Blood & Honour, banned far-right organisations such as National Socialists Chemnitz, and far-right movements such as PEGIDA.

The racist riots were framed as silent marches in remembrance of the victim – who was neither a member nor a sympathiser of any of the protesting far-right groups. But they can be interpreted as 'the outcome of long-term developments in Saxony'.[8] For decades, the city of Chemnitz had been a breeding ground for the far-right scene and its subcultural structures.[9] The far-right terrorist group National Socialist Underground (Nationalsozialistischer Untergrund, NSU) had found a significant network of supporters in Chemnitz and Zwickau where it had existed clandestinely for years during which time it committed murders and nail bomb attacks against migrants, robbed banks and designed and sold Nazi versions of Monopoly via an internet platform.

Whilst the 2018 Chemnitz riots were internationally the most visible far-right riots, racist riots and fire-bombings of asylum centres have been happening all over Saxony since 2015 – most notably in Freital, Bautzen, Heidenau and Claussnitz – while new terrorist sovereigntist organisations such as Revolution Chemnitz and Gruppe Freital were founded (both prosecuted as a terrorist organisation as they were not successfully clandestine). The expert on the German far-right Hajo Funke explains that Nazis have been networking in and around Chemnitz for decades, and that he regards the local Nazi subculture of mobs, vigilante groups and right-wing fraternities to be so strong and well organised that he expected a right-wing terrorist revolution to come from there.[10] Against this background, the 2018 Chemnitz riots are not a one-off event. They are just the tip of the iceberg (see Figure 2.1).

The instant organising was so successful partly because the homicide was a trigger event that stimulated an already

Figure 2.1 AfD demonstration in Erfurt, 1 May 2019.

intertwined network of far-right groups to act, including hooligans, neo-Nazis and unorganised sympathisers. The far right uses homicides, rapes or threatening behaviour by visible minorities to mobilise centrists.[11] The figure of the violent male Muslim migrant serves as a cipher. For some, the migrant is a figure of unfair geographical and social mobility;[12] other focus more on the preservation of 'our' culture, allegedly endangered by the influx of others; some worry about the rights of indigenous workers whose wage expectations are undermined by ever cheaper waves of migrants.[13] The far right thus succeeds in rallying so-called 'ordinary citizens' to express 'their anger about the killing and Germany's asylum policy'.[14] As the American sociologist Cynthia Miller-Idriss noted, the closing of ranks between a variety of far-right groups and 'ordinary citizens' might be regarded as a new development, yet has to be contextualised, especially in regard to post-reunification developments – politically, economically, socially – in Eastern Germany, as one might come to the conclusion that the situation is coming to its head.[15]

As we have shown elsewhere, until the racist riots of Chemnitz in 2018, two particular types of far-right street protests were predominant in Germany: 'first, marches by militant neo-Nazis, far-right hooligans, or New Right groups such as the Identitarian Movement, that were numerically small and occurred infrequently; and second, larger far-right anti-Islam PEGIDA marches that attracted thousands of "ordinary people" in Germany since 2014'.[16] Cynthia Miller-Idriss argued that with the murder in Chemnitz as a trigger event, these two types came together, and in effect far-right militants and activists were joined by 'ordinary people' and elected AfD representatives. She concluded:

A third sector of the extreme right-wing – the leaders of right-wing political parties like the Alternative for Germany (*AfD*, now the third largest party in federal parliament) – and local elites added fuel to the fire by celebrating the Chemnitz protesters as revolutionaries, framing the riots as justifiable resistance that signalled the beginning of the end of a corrupt state. Extreme right-wing leaders even compared the riots to the youth- and citizen-led democratic protests of 1968 and 1989. This rhetoric further empowered ordinary citizens and legitimized the violence.[17]

Referencing the 1968 political uprisings and the 1989 peaceful revolution proved to be a powerful strategy to elicit an atmosphere of revolution and of resistance against a regime framed as authoritarian or even totalitarian, fuelling the affective energies of the protests ultimately expressed as rage and anger about the murder, and more importantly, about the political decisions of 'the establishment' concerning immigration and asylum policies.[18] Language of revolution is in the air, and not just amongst sectarian racists.

During our observations of the Chemnitz riots, the protesters' use of the resistance topos was striking:

On 9 November 2018 – an important and controversial date in the recent history of Germany, as it commemorates both the November Pogroms in 1938 and the fall of the Berlin wall in 1989 – Pro Chemnitz chose to organise a far-right demonstration, and, once again, racist activists from a variety of organisations stood next to 'ordinary', 'worried citizens', chanting 'Resistance!' in unison. People gathered in front of the Chemnitz Karl Marx memorial that evening, and families with children stood next to men wearing T-shirts with identifiable neo-Nazi codes and martial arts club logos. Many people seemed to know each other; the atmosphere was friendly, people were engaging in small talk, and expressing feelings of belonging and a shared community [...]. The assembled crowd cheered and chanted, waved their flags – German flags and those of the different far-right groups' symbols. The organisers shouted: '[... Stand up] for our homeland! We just have this one homeland!' The crowd cheered: [...] 'Resistance! Resistance!' And the organisers shouted: 'Together we shall overthrow the government!' [... and] 'The system is at its end! We are the turning point!' 'Merkel has to go!' 'Resistance! Resistance!'[19]

The summer of 2018 thus saw the comeback of one of the worst aspects of life in the East: the return of public affrays, pogroms and racist demonstrations that had been so common after the 'peaceful' revolution in 1989. These were not and are not spontaneous events, as this chapter shows. One of the aims of far-right splinter groups is to take over the public sphere in Eastern Germany by taking over urban spaces through highly visible 'peace marches' (against migrants), 'silent marches' (on the occasion of violence by refugees) and demonstrations commemorating 'the slaughter of Dresden' in 1945. Pogroms are not always publicly organised, however, though they are never as spontaneous as their defenders claim. They are demonstrations of power, they are intended to undermine the state's monopoly over the legitimate use of force, and they serve to intimidate the left and liberal members of civil society.

Signal incidents involving homicide and sexual violence by stigmatised minorities are frequently triggers whenever the far right successfully mobilises significant political grassroots movements. This is not accidental. For such events provide a bridge between personal fears of violence and projections of a threatening alien force, linking the personal anxiety with the political interpretation that German society, imagined as overwhelmingly peaceful, is infiltrated by potent and brutal intruders against whom 'the liberals' are unwilling to protect us. Thus, such incidents increase the plausibility of far-right narratives of alien invaders by providing a genial reduction of complexity and by stoking further fears of a decline of order, civilisation, peace and general cultural demise.[20] Single events can be used to crystallise personal affects and allow them to be combined with large-scale narratives of doom – a perfect catalyst for mobilising significantly different social groups.

The sentiment of impending doom galvanises resistance fighters. The capacities for mobilising rage and anti-establishment resentment are grounded in what we have termed the far right's 'master narrative of resistance'. Social and collective actions are framed as acts of resistance; voicing anger, marching in the streets and even attacking other people are seen as urgent and necessary, if these actions serve to perform resistance against 'the system', 'the establishment', the 'old parties' etc. in order to defend 'the nation', 'the homeland', 'the people' against the imminent 'Muslim invasion'. The survival of the nation's 'natural order' is allegedly threatened by a 'Great replacement' and all those responsible for it – which allows for the blaming of politicians, elites, journalists, liberals and practically all those people who allegedly know what's going on, but are lying to the people about it. Thus, the threat is situated both on the outside of the imagined community – the 'murderers of the people' (*Volksmörder*) – and on the inside – the 'traitors of the people' (*Volksverräter*).

Such talk is taken up by a particularly unabashedly right-wing section of the AfD, the spokesperson of which is Björn Höcke. In 2018, in one of the infamous Kyffhäuser meetings, Höcke appealed to the audience: 'The Germans have to ask themselves and decide whether they want to be hammer or anvil, that was the question raised by Bernhard von Bülow in 1899.' Bernhard von Bülow (1849–1929), the Chancellor of the German Reich from 1900 to 1909, had addressed the Reichstag in a speech in 1899 in which he argued for a 'greater Germany' and an expansionary foreign policy, ultimately asking the Germans if they wanted to be 'hammer' or 'anvil' – in other words, if they wanted to beat or be beaten.[21] Höcke, in 2018, continued: 'Today, dear friends, the question is no longer hammer or anvil. The question today is sheep or wolf. And I – no, we – decide under these circumstances to be wolf!' The audience burst into applause. Höcke concluded that 'the time of acceptance', 'the time of patience', 'the *time of the sheep*' will soon be 'over once and for all!'[22]

The wolf/sheep analogy has been a recurring cipher in German politics. Most notably, Joseph Goebbels (1897–1945), the Reich Minister of Propaganda of Nazi Germany from 1933 to 1945, used the wolf metaphor in one of the articles he wrote for the NSDAP journal *The Attack* (*Der Angriff*) before the Reichstag elections in 1928. Goebbels stated that

> We enter the Reichstag to arm ourselves with democracy's weapons. We are joining the Reichstag MPs to paralyse the Weimar disposition with its own endorsement. If democracy is foolish enough to give us free railway passes and salaries, that is its problem. We are not worried ... We shall use all lawful means to revolutionise today's condition. We come neither as friends nor as neutrals. We come as enemies! As the wolf attacks the sheep, so come we.[23]

Höcke's quotation is often related to that of Goebbels, and yet: Höcke was lamenting the fact that a teenager had taken a beating at a school playground, and that he had not learned self-defence or even to fight. So Höcke was in fact referring to German teenagers as sheep, contrasting them to migrant teenagers as wolves, and lamenting that division of social roles – and wishing for a state of affairs in which Germans

are more wolflike. Goebbels referred to the national socialists as wolves and the Weimar democrats as sheep. The metaphors thus stand for different social analyses, what they both
have in common is an admiration for the wolf – reflecting
the National Socialists' totemic identification with large
predators, as Boria Sax argues.[24] As a totem animal and an
animal that stands for the Nazis and their propensity to violence, the wolf stands for 'pride, tenacity, cunning',[25] and as
such both are particularly dangerous to 'us' if the wolf comes
from the outside, and particularly dangerous to others if 'we'
manage to be the wolves. The wolf as National Socialist
totem has its origin in Nordic myths, and, as such, was an
object of fascination in the Third Reich, in particular to Adolf
Hitler, who named two of his headquarters Wolfsschlucht
and Wolfsschanze.[26] Even today, some far-right organisations refer to themselves as wolves, for instance the Division
Braune Wölfe (Division Brown Wolves), an organisation that
has been classified as terrorist by the Federal Office for the
Protection of Constitution.

And yet Höcke's wishes for a more 'wolfish' politics are
being fulfilled by the rioters and the 'ordinary citizens' in
Chemnitz. The wolves are returning, fascism is, again, on
the rise. But this kind of wolf has always been an integral
part of postwar history of both Germanys. In other words,
attacks on groups deemed 'weaker than us' have always
been an integral part of these histories. The early 1990s, the
first years of a new and united Germany, witnessed a sudden
rise in racist attacks and racist violence that were in 'the
eyes of many [...] reminiscent of the 1920s and early 1930s',
the historian Mary Fulbrook explains.[27] In September 1991,
nco-Nazi pogroms on buildings inhabited by refugees and
international contract labourers lasted for several days
in the Saxon town Hoyerswerda. The violence escalated

because of the weakness of local law enforcement, and the violence-supporting applause of, yet again, the 'ordinary' citizens of Hoyerswerda.[28] After several days, the refugees were evacuated at their own request. Outside their shelter, they had put a placard for the world to see: 'Why do you hate us? SOS. We have been living in fear for many days. We want to go back to Western Germany. Western Germany only.'[29] In Eastern Germany, the pogroms of Hoyerswerda in 1991 and the pogroms of Rostock-Lichtenhagen in 1992, in which about a thousand Nazis took part, have been the most visible in public debate.[30] Yet racist attacks occurred in Western Germany as well, for instance in the towns of Solingen and Mölln, where arson attacks on buildings inhabited by Turkish families killed many. However, they were conducted at night, in the absence of a cheering public. In Hoyerswerda and Rostock, the attacks on the homes for refugees and contract labourers occurred over several days and under frenetic applause and cheering of 'ordinary citizens' who gathered for elaborate picnics while watching the attacks.[31]

In the whole of Germany incidents of racist violence increased in the early 1990s, including racist and anti-Semitic attacks, attacks on people with disabilities, on gay and trans people, lesbians and sex workers, and desecrations of Jewish cemeteries increased.[32] These attacks were 'basically directed at any people designated as "outsiders" to "Germany" – encapsulated in the slogan: "Germany for the Germans"'.[33]

Most observers agree that the pogroms of the early 1990s were not entirely new developments. Fulbrook noted that there had been a rise of far-right violence in Western Germany on the one hand at least since the mid-1970s that manifested in an increase of attacks on migrants, in particular on visible migrants framed as 'guest workers' (*Gastarbeiter*) from Mediterranean countries, while Chancellor Helmut Kohl 'continued to assert that "Germany is not a country of immigration"'.[34] On the other hand, although Eastern Germany had only a few migrant workers from Cuba, Vietnam, Mozambique and Poland, and although the GDR was a self-proclaimed 'anti-fascist state', neo-Nazis there increasingly became an issue in the 1980s – being a neo-Nazi, Fulbrook explained, was framed as an act of resistance against the state of the GDR:

> So to express rebellion against the state, people might naturally choose the symbols to which the state was most hostile. To flaunt a swastika in the GDR in the 1980s was less to hark back to Hitler than to demonstrate against Honecker. Right-wing skinheads and hooligans were a home-grown product of the GDR, not a flashback to the Third Reich; and they were an increasing problem in the 1980s, long before anyone dreamed that the Wall might fall. In the volatile circumstances since unification, these elements have come together and been transformed.[35]

Many scholars have explained the pogroms in the early 1990s as associated with the political, economic and social turmoil that accompanied the process of Germany's unification. Others point towards the continuities of racist violence in both Eastern and Western Germany, where pogrom-like attacks have been happening since the 1970s. In fact, the first pogrom in Germany since the end of the Second World War took place in August 1975 in Erfurt, the capital of Thuringia, where Eastern German racists chased a group of Algerians across the entire city for several days.[36] When the Wall came down and the GDR disappeared, the Eastern German neo-Nazis and racists remained, and they no longer had to hide the fact that they were, indeed, neo-Nazis.

Historians of the early 1990s all describe how the far-right scene thrived and flourished all over Eastern Germany, how it took over public spaces in smaller towns and in rural areas, and how it established itself as local authorities of public order. The pogroms in Hoyerswerda and other cities were mass events of the far right.[37] Such events might very well serve to explain the hopes of neo-Nazis of taking over the republic, as they are read in retrospect as symptoms of the weakness of the state and its imminent demise.[38] Thus, the East has seen a flourishing of militant far-right terrorists, a cohort of 'lone wolves', which culminated in the series of terrorist attacks by the NSU in the early 2000s. Observers even argue that the far-right milieux that have been proliferating throughout Eastern Germany since the GDR help explain the levels of racist rioting against refugees and migrants happening today.[39] In other words, the foundations for the 2018 racist riots in Chemnitz have been laid out by the 'Generation Hoyerswerda'.[40]

Every one of these pogroms and pogrom-like events can be regarded as a demonstration of power by a rising backdrop of far-right activists, terrorists and plotters against state authorities. Besides documented and reported incidents we know of a plethora of everyday micro-political acts of aggression that remain unreported. The small Saxon town Colditz is a case in point. Here, a far-right kinship clan associated with the timber industry terrorise their neighbours. Ralf Neuber, his sons and their friends chase more liberal and leftist Colditzians, organise parties at his house with shouts of 'Sieg Heil' reverberating across the village and commit arson attacks against houses in which Turkish families live. They also, it appears, run the local meth trade.[41] Under the influence of Ralf Neuber's family, Colditz has increasingly become a lawless area.[42]

When a group of about a hundred neo-Nazi youths terror-
ised the town centre in 2008, chasing residents and smash-
ing in windows of local businesses, the police telephone
records show that despite increasingly desperate pleas for
help by local citizens, tourists and small business owners,
the officers remained non-reactive for hours.[43] Some small
towns in rural areas remain tightly in the grip of neo-Nazis
who, so it seems, successfully restore the order of 'their'
municipality in accordance with their views of good order.
In larger conurbations like Leipzig, anti-fascist activities are much more successful in keeping the far right's
power demonstrations at bay. But many smaller towns and
rural areas remain exposed to the far right's takeovers of
public space, and the far-right operatives remain largely
unopposed.[44]

Today's far-right agents legitimise their activities not
just with references to blood and honour, anti-Muslim
rhetoric and references to the Germans dying out. They
also argue their case with reference to the German constitution. Thor von Waldstein, a lawyer specialising in inland
water navigation, distinguishes the current inhabitants of
Germany ('federal Germans') from 'true Germans'. A true
German is, he argues in an interview with the right-wing
magazine *Sezession* in 2015, a German who 'feels more
connected to the memory of his ancestors and the future
of his children than the ephemeral chichi sentimentali-
ties of many of his contemporaries'.[45] These Germans feel
as if they lived in the 'wrong state', he argues. In fact, he
says, the Federal Republic is merely a type of interregnum
ordered by 'Trizonia', the members of the occupying forces
after the war. According to him, the task is thus to remove
this interregnum and work towards a 'real' German government by Germans for Germans (of the real kind, whatever

that means).[46] This goal is best achieved, Waldstein argues, with the help of the constitution, of which article 20 states that:

(1) The Federal Republic of Germany is a democratic and social federal state.
(2) All state authority is derived from the people. It shall be exercised by the people through elections and other votes and through specific legislative, executive and judicial bodies.
(3) The legislature shall be bound by the constitutional order, the executive and the judiciary by law and justice.
(4) All Germans shall have the right to resist any person seeking to abolish this constitutional order if no other remedy is available.[47]

The 'culture of welcome' for the Syrian war refugees in 2015 and 2016 constitutes just the sort of situation in which resistance is legitimate, according to Waldstein. The welcome of the refugees is seen as an attempt to 'abolish this constitutional order'. This fits in with various far-right conspiracy theories whereby an international conspiracy of Jews are trying to take control by replacing the current population with another, more malleable, ethnically different population – basically, Germans are exchanged for sub-Saharan Africans and migrants from the Middle East who will submit more gullibly (so goes the narrative) to the manipulations of 'Jews'. The far-right magazine *Compact* illustrates this hypothesis with a depiction of George Soros, puppet master, manipulating Angela Merkel (see Figure 2.2).

The government, in Waldstein's view, is aiming to turn Germany into a land of diversity and heterogeneity and thereby perpetrating 'acts of racism against its own people', by turning Germany into an ethnic and religious melting pot. This is a coup d'état from above, argues Waldstein.

Figure 2.2 George Soros, puppet master of Angela Merkel, on the cover of *Compact* magazine.

Of course, resistance is the only recourse. In particular, as other far-right publicists argue, the government is waging battles in the East of the country in which 'ethnic German homogeneity' is still the norm. To some degree, this is quite a successful narrative in Eastern Germany. This part of the country has in fact seen much lower levels of migration than the West, and those migrant workers who had been invited through intergovernmental contracts were mostly recalled or sent back in 1990.[48] The lack of diversity is now being framed by the far right as an exciting new opportunity for territorialising the 'right way' of being German.

The rise of the East: prophets of another Germany

On 6 July 2019 members of the AfD met in Leinefelde, a small town in the north of Thuringia, on the occasion of the fifth Kyffhäuser meeting – an annual event organised by Der Flügel, the *völkisch* wing of the AfD. 'Kyffhäuser' is the name of a Thuringian range of mountains, where, according to a well-known German myth, Emperor Frederick I, Holy Roman Emperor until 1190 and commonly known as Barbarossa, 'lies sleeping' until the country needs him. When he returns, he eliminates all forms of injustice. This myth is recycled to justify the activities of the Flügel: a resurrection that will achieve justice.[49]

In front of an audience of several hundred AfD members and supporters, Björn Höcke stood below a banner: 'The East arises'. His speech begins: 'We are back in Thuringia, and this makes me – as the state party leader – tremendously proud, because the Free State Thuringia, the green heart of Germany, fulfills all the prerequisites to become an AfD core state.'[50] The Thuringians, Höcke explains, have a particularly close relationship with their homeland, and it is also the 'state of fear' for the Green party, which is not really getting a foot on the ground in regional elections. Still, 'the climate hype has touched the Germans,' he said, 'and the Germans, unfortunately, are not just an obedient, sheep-like people, but a bit hysterical, too,' and thus would be particularly sensitive to the Green 'hypermoralists' and the 'climate hysteria', he explained. The Germans need to 'wake up'. Eastern Germans at least had experienced the dictatorship of the GDR, and are consequently more sensitive to dictatorial developments, he argues. They had overthrown an unjust system once before, and they could, and should, do it again. The revolution, he implies, begins here and spreads to the rest of the Republic, a revolution that will begin with the regional elections of 2019: 'In Saxony and Brandenburg, and six weeks later in Thuringia, we will let the political sun rise again over the East, and we will make sure that this sun will illuminate the whole of Germany, that common sense will rule again, that natural patriotism will regain old grounds,' to the audience standing up, clapping and shouting. The political sun rises in the East, for a change, it is what people like to hear.

Björn Höcke presents himself as the prophet of another Germany. Within the AfD, he has found support in the *völkisch* wing and has succeeded in constructing a space in which his *völkisch* nationalist vision for a new German identity can thrive. For the AfD and its (former) splinter parties such as the ADPM, the East has become an object of projection (see Figure 2.3).[51] Right-wing politicians are trying to reinvent the East for the purpose of gaining votes. Such an approach makes them attractive to people who have been suffering from a long tradition of bashing Eastern Germans.[52] Yet in recent years the Eastern German

Figure 2.3 Election placard by ADPM.

identity has developed into a political battleground, and far-right politicians have discovered that such an identity can be reinvented. Collective identities are always malleable and can become a subject of political strategy. Collectively,

AfD politicians are trying to reinvent the East as a region of national resistance, and they argue that the Eastern Germans are more sensitive to systemic injustice and totalitarian regimes. Ending his speech in the 2019 'Kyffhäuser' meeting, Höcke raised his voice to appeal to the audience:

> Here in the East, we have had our personal experiences with a totalitarian society. And with our personal experiences with this totalitarian society [...] we are facing the barbarism of prohibition and paternalism dominating the West. Yes, dear friends, it feels like being back in the GDR, but together, we will make this promise today: We won't be led into a new GDR ever again, we won't submit! [...] Long live Thuringia! Long live our German fatherland! Long live the real Europe! The East arises! Let's get our nation back!

In Leinefelde that day, the audience was standing up, applauding, shouting and waving German flags, and then they started to chant in unison, 'Höcke! Höcke! Höcke!' Here, at least, the politician's attempt at reinventing and reclassifying a collective identity – inherently 'awake' and 'resistant', inherently 'wolf' – clearly resonated with the attending audience.

The 'GIDA' movements (organisations founded in the shadow of PEGIDA) have been taking the same approach to emphasise the East's superiority over Western Germany: Eastern Germans, they claim on the one hand, have a more nuanced sense of justice, recognise injustice more easily and are more likely to resist injustices than Western Germans – who, on the other hand, are more likely to be ideologically indoctrinated by an ominous 'system'. A representative of THÜGIDA told us in an interview: 'Thuringia and Saxony are somewhat like Gaul [as in: Asterix and Obelix resisting the Romans] where resistance is, in part, still being carried out.' He explained that Germany is being 'brainwashed', and Western Germans have been 're-educated' to make them entirely passive followers. 'Here' (in the East) however, 'it is still obvious to everyone that we must rise up against injustice'.[53]

In an AfD campaigning event in the small Saxon town Grosspösna, Jörg Urban, the state party leader in Saxony, told the audience that he would feel 'pity' for their Western German AfD colleagues, because

> They act in an environment in which everybody has been thoroughly stultified – *for decades*! But here, the people don't believe what the papers are writing. Thirty years ago, at least some older people experienced that everyone was brazenly lying. So, we know what that is like. And our colleagues [in the West] are trying their best, because they don't want to watch how the country is going down the drain. In Saxony, we actually live in the Garden of Eden compared to Western Germany. A quarter of the people already vote for us here! So, we can be a little bit more courageous.[54]

For both AfD and PEGIDA, the journal *Compact – Magazine for Sovereignty* provides good copy. In 2017, *Compact* published a themed issue with the title 'Shining Eastern Germany. What the West needs to be taught' (*Der Osten leuchtet. Was der Westen lernen kann*). On the cover, the picture of a blonde woman with piercing blue eyes and the colours of the German flag painted across her shoulders beamingly smiles into the distance.

In one of the issue's articles titled 'The Unleashed West', the New Right publicist Manfred Kleine-Hartlage opines, 'Eastern Germany is the bastion of common sense.'[55] Half a century since the beginning of 'mass migration of Muslims to Europe', he argued, they would not have made any progress in terms of integration. 'When Islamic communities stabilise successfully to the detriment of their non-Muslim environment, this is not merely due to the nature of Islam, but due to the environment that puts up with the destabilising activities of Islam.' He implies that Western Germany suffers most from an ongoing 'Islamisation', and concurrently criticises the Western Germans, writing that 'a downright grotesque self-delusion of Green-voting, liberal, tolerant, gender-sensitive, gay-rights-focused multiculturalists and do-gooders insists on believing that anyone who is not entirely off their head wants to be like them. Their own ridiculousness is only hidden, because their ideologically contaminated media pats them on the back.'[56]

He concludes that Western Germans are 'neurotics who impose their neuroses on the nation and thereby lead it to perdition'. In contrast, the Eastern states 'summon considerably more resistance than the Western ones because two social concepts were tested on German soil after 1945'. One was liberalism, which leads to ever more demands once its goals have been reached, and another was the attempt to realise a concrete utopia that had to turn conservative. In sum, he valorises an Eastern German collective identity: 'Mainstream journalists often ask gloatingly, why the East, where so few foreigners live, is so vehemently against immigration. The correct if undesirable answer is that the Germans east of the Elbe still have common sense and have no interest in becoming like the aforementioned green-voting hacks, multiculturalists and do-gooders.'[57]

According to this author of the New Right, and to other authors appearing in the themed issue of *Compact*, Eastern Germans are still able to resist the beginning of the 'replacement' of the 'German people'. Martin Müller-Mertens titled his contribution to the issue 'That a decent German nation/ Flourish as do other lands' (*Dass ein gutes Deutschland blühe*)[58] a quotation from a poem by Bertolt Brecht called

'Children's hymn' (*Kinderhymne*) written as a response to
the Western German national hymn.[59] Even today, Müller-
Mertens opines, 'the East is more patriotic'. As Western
Germany was occupied by US forces after the Second
World War, the people were, for many decades, affected by
'US-guided re-education', 'postnational Westernisation' and
'the national nihilism of the political Left'. 'The bottom
line is,' Müller-Mertens writes, 'that in retaining patriotism and love for the home country, Eastern Germany of the
1980s was characterised by the renaissance of regionalism,
in particular in Thuringia and in Saxony. Those are the very
regions characterised by the greatest resistance against the
great replacement and Islamisation.' To him, the PEGIDA
demonstrations are proof of this. He describes these heroi-
cally as 'the last line of defence' against the invading
hordes: 'Whilst the West was overrun by invaders operating
under the guise of asylum, a grassroots pushback formed
in the East. The West German establishment reacted with
incomprehension, resentments, even hatred against the
Dunkeldeutschland in the East.'[60]

Instead of discussing the political demands of the PEGIDA
movement, Western Germans use the term 'Nazi' to ver-
bally cudgel 'dissenters', and the term 'Dunkeldeutsche'
('dark Germans') to pillory the whole region, he argues.
Dunkeldeutschland can be translated as 'dark Germany',
and is a pejorative and negative term used to describe
Eastern Germany since the 1990s. *Dunkeldeutschland* was
then and is now associated with backwardness, xenopho-
bia, violence against 'Others' and right-wing extremism. 'A
bright new Germany shines against the dark Germany' was
a quotation from Joachim Gauck, former German President,
in August 2015. At the same time, *Dunkeldeutschland* was
used as the title for an issue of *Der Spiegel*, the cover of

which depicted a brightly burning house against the night sky.[61] The daily *Hamburger Morgenpost* showed Saxony as a brown blemish on the German map, and a Germany without Saxony was envisioned, coining the satirical term *Säxit* in analogy to the British Brexit.[62]

Since then, the New Right has found a way to make political use of the declassifications of Eastern Germany. In his second piece, Müller-Mertens explains that, for the longest time, Eastern Germany was deemed to be 'the *Mezzogiorno* of Germany', underdeveloped, corrupt, a little medieval but with nice landscapes like the south of Italy. Yet since the 'catastrophe' of migrants 'flooding our country', Müller-Mertens argues, the East will have to take on a new role – as the last 'bastion' against the 'exchange of the population', 'Islamisation' and the problems involved with a 'politically correct re-education'. So the AfD and the magazine *Compact* are putting a positive spin on the deindustrialisation: because there have been no jobs to be had for a long time, and there are still few well-paid positions, it is very rare for people to migrate to this part of the country. Out of this, they make an argument that this is a purer segment of the country, which in turn justifies the revolution rising in the East.

Such insurrectionist logics are found outside of magazine articles. For the German national holiday on 3 October 2018, a demonstration by a new movement called We for Germany (Wir für Deutschland) took place in downtown Berlin. The protestors could be heard to chant 'We are the people' (*Wir sind das Volk*). The counter-demonstration, meanwhile, shielded by a great number of police officers in riot gear, was chanting 'Germany never again' (*Nie wieder Deutschland*), which is one of the slogans of the anti-Germans (more about this in Chapter 4). Huge black flags with white lettering in Gothic letters said: 'Widerstand lässt sich nicht verbieten', which means 'You cannot prohibit resistance'. 'We are the resistance', the protestors kept chanting, and 'You cannot get rid of us'. Some placards read threateningly 'Chemnitz is everywhere', implying that the Chemnitz riots were just the beginning of a civil war that they were about to start – an oblique way of uttering threats without criminalising themselves. We heard the protestors droning in unison, over and over: 'Those who do not love Germany, should leave Germany' (*Wer Deutschland nicht liebt, soll Deutschland verlassen*) and, even more hauntingly, 'Awaken, Germany! Victory to Germany' (*Deutschland erwache, Deutschland den Sieg*). One flag we have come to know from the PEGIDA demonstrations in Dresden, the 'Wirmer flag' showing a black and yellow cross on a red background, is associated with the National Socialist resistance fighter Josef Wirmer (1901–44) and used to symbolise the fight against the Hitler regime. Yet since 1999 the flag has been appropriated by German far-right groups, among them the German Defence League, Hooligans against Salafism (HOGESA) and PEGIDA. The far-right news portal Politically Incorrect states that the Wirmer flag symbolises the act of resisting 'foreign rule'.[63] These demonstrators are presenting themselves as the face of resistance against a new form of fascism which they call 'liberal fascism'. In referencing Stauffenberg and the other people of the resistance in the Nazi Reich who were standing on the side of the good against evil, they are implying that this is what they are doing: repeating history by resisting a new fascist regime that is hell-bent on destroying Germany.[64] The topos of resistance and the figure of the migrant are both unifying features of the otherwise fragmented far-right organisations, parties and lone wolves. In

Chemnitz the crowds chanted 'Resistance, resistance!' even as they chased visible minorities through the city centre on those hot late summer days: The people interpreted as being migrants, left-wing or gay embody the faults of the system, they signify the functioning of the dictatorship allegedly replacing Germans with foreigners.

The new conservative and right-wing parties are using such narratives of resistance. In the 2019 regional elections, the AfD won 27.5 per cent of the vote in Saxony, 23.4 per cent in Thuringia and 23.5 per cent in Brandenburg.[65] A quarter of voters thus voted for this ultra-conservative party in 2019, a party that is notorious for its difficulties in reining in MPs who make openly racist public statements. Some examples of the most high-profile statements of this kind are:

- AfD front-runner Alexander Gauland said in June 2018: 'Hitler and the Nazis are a mere trifle in a thousand years of successful German history'; earlier he had called the German national footballer Jérôme Boateng the sort of foreigner nobody wants as a neighbour.
- The AfD MP Jens Maier called the son of a formerly successful tennis player 'a runty blackamoor'.
- Thomas Göbel, an AfD candidate who spoke at a PEGIDA event in Dresden in June 2016, sees Germany as subject to 'an infestation of parasitic vermin and freeloaders' who 'gorge themselves on the flesh of German bones'.
- Thomas Seitz, AfD candidate for Emmendingen-Lahr, calls the Prophet Muhammad a 'sadistic blood guzzler and nonce'.
- Many AfD politicians see the Greens and the Merkel government as infiltrated and manipulated by the 'New World Order'.[66]

It is easy to dismiss such utterances as those of wanton provocateurs fishing on the fringes of the far right and the fringes of esoteric conspiracy theories. What is clear is that the scandalised reactions by mainstream media are not putting off voters, for the very reason that many see the defamations as a conspiracy of the establishment, backed by the media, to scandalise issues without focusing on what really matters: anti-migrant, pro-German politics really does galvanise the crowds in Eastern Germany.

Young AfD voters in particular point to its anti-immigrant, anti-Islamic statements as making the party particularly attractive to them, according to journalistic reports.[67] But the vast majority of voters are claiming that the AfD is attractive since it is currently the only party that is considered opposed to the establishment. For instance, the AfD is the one party that opposed the chancellor's migration policies in 2015 and 2016, and this was the most frequently given reason for voting for that party.[68] This has changed: the federal government has amended the policy of open doors and signed over millions of Euros in exchange for Turkey closing the border to Syrians wanting to move west; only a tiny trickle of refugee migrants are now crossing into German territory.

The AfD is on a winning streak, however. In the 2019 election campaign it emphasised wolf politics in rural areas of Eastern Germany, agitated against the 'establishment' and enacted itself as a socialist party that is decidedly welfare-chauvinist, that is it wants to distribute welfare only to German citizens deemed deserving enough. This is an attractive position to many, as our own research is showing. In 2018 and 2019 we conducted 150 group interviews in four German regions, and have found nationalist welfare chauvinism prevalent across different party preferences, regions and age groups.[69] The poor have to be deserving, and part of what it means to be deserving is to make an effort to work, not have 'too many' children and have a certain background, as some people could not, even if they wanted, become deserving, many of our respondents claim. Those who are undeserving should, if of migrant extraction, leave German territory – and so should many Germans. German nationalism is thus turning into an achievement of what is deserved, rather than an achievement by descent, and is approximating narratives found elsewhere concerning what it means to be a good American, for instance.[70] Whilst these attitudes are widespread, the AfD is the only party that currently makes a policy out of such fantasies of exclusion: it successfully regroups the disaffected through a politics of resentment. In fact, of all voters, it is the voters of the AfD who are most critical of federal politics.[71]

Saxony is in Eastern Europe, Germany is in Saxony

One person's freedom fighter is the next person's terrorist. One person's excrement on a map is the next person's beacon of white hope.

'Ex Oriente Lux', Light from the East, as the publicist Adolph Przybyszewski put it in a special edition of the New Right magazine *Sezession* on the topic of Saxony[72]

Saxony, the state most often portrayed as the heart of *Dunkeldeutschland*, is, according to the leading New Right figure Götz Kubitschek, also the centre of resistance against the 'disintegration of everything by postmodern arbitrariness'.[73] The self-anointed leader of a far-right think-tank praises Saxony's simple workers who doggedly and shrewdly hold against the moderns and the postmodernists. Many of the recent scandals for which Eastern Germany has become known have taken place in Saxony. A range of explanations is offered: the authoritarianism of the GDR, deficits in democratisation, racisms, defiance against the establishment, the prewar voting behaviour, the closeness to external borders.[74] Saxons are also most likely to be victims of an anti-Saxon racism, unironically called 'Säxism'. Thus, the conservative journalist Seidel argues, the Saxon love for the homeland is a source of pride and of suffering, while the Saxon becomes the scapegoat for all that is going wrong in Germany.[75]

This leads the former priest and former leader in the Eastern Germany resistance movement Frank Richter to ask in his book title, *Is Saxony Still Part of Germany?* He argues that the demise of the GDR left a wounded people – wounded in their pride, in their wallets, in their ability to govern their own affairs.[76] The 1989 revolution could have been a source of great pride: finally, the Eastern Germans had peacefully achieved something of historical importance, and yet this great achievement was snatched from them by overbearing Western Germans bringing a poisoned chalice, as we saw in the first chapter.

From an international perspective, Saxony's neighbouring countries to the East – Poland and the Czech Republic – have had a longer history of being governed by conservative nationalist parties for a number of reasons, including weak loyalty to democratic institutions, low party membership, a roll-back of welfare in the midst of economic crises and rampant deindustrialisation, as the political scientist Michael Minkenberg has shown.[77] The Eastern German states share some of these social features, though the roll-back of the welfare state was not as harsh, and the economic collapse allowed options for mobile individuals. But can the rise of the right in Germany be explained in post-socialist terms?

The Eastern territories share features with other post-socialist countries that have developed strong radical right movements and political parties, as Minkenberg has shown. The dominant pattern, he argues, is

> national identity without the nation-state, that is an ethno-cultural nationhood, and the establishment of a nation-state along with rapid democratization after World War I, soon to be replaced by authoritarian dictatorships in the interwar period and communist regimes after World War II. These are region-specific legacies shared by most countries in Eastern Europe and with relevance to the radical right. Moreover, while in Western Europe immigrants take the role of scapegoats, these are not readily available in Eastern Europe; instead, national minorities and neighboring countries take this position.[78]

Thus, the efforts of nation-building are not deemed to have been successfully ended, and grassroots and political movements fill in the unfinished developments by over-emphasising and in the process producing a kitschy version of the allegedly ancient nation. They proclaim nostalgia for the old despotic regimes and the ethnic and territorial conception of national identity that prevailed under them, following the nation-building struggles before and after the First World War.[79]

As the far-right magazine *Compact* argued in September 2018, just after the Chemnitz riots, the ideal would be a secession from Germany and a new white nationalist enclave free of Muslims.[80] According to this perspective, the ideal development is for Eastern Germany and Bavaria to secede from Germany to make a separate white ethnic state, while Sunnis and Shiites will divide up the Western territories in different spheres of influence. The north-west will unite with the 'Caliphate of Antwerp' and will organise into an Islamic Federation; the south-west will turn into the

Sunni-dominated German Caliphate. Finally, the authors say that the (Eastern) German Republic will close its borders to the West and unite with Eastern Europe and Austria. The Eastern European countries build a white enclave, free of the dangers of Islam, and free of the impertinences associated with immigrants.[81] Far-right circles imagine Eastern Germany as a beacon of white nationalism, separate from the 'degenerate' West and in a natural co-operation with Eastern Europe and Austria, equally imagined as white, Christian and gender-conservative.

Markus Roscher-Meinel, whose tweet handle is 'lawyerberlin', tweeted in 2017 that Muslims have replaced the local populations in the West, and those who have not moved to the real Germany (i.e. Eastern Germany) in time would have to apply for asylum there. 'Patriots from the caliphate will be given preferential treatment in their asylum application,' he tweets, hashtag 'irony' (see Figure 2.4). But versions of this map, sometimes including the Netherlands or Bavaria in the 'caliphate', and Poland in the 'real Germany', have been circulating for years.

The political standing of Saxony, and of the Eastern German states in general, remains complicated. Eastern Germany does have a different past from Western Germany, but a narrative of this past, how it frames the present and how it might project into the future, is largely omitted from the national narratives of the Federal Republic of Germany. Events such as the 2018 Chemnitz riots and pogroms act like triggers to the struggle of which narrative we should tell about the East – while, for many observers, these pogrom-like incidents are a validation of the *Dunkeldeutschland* narrative that has prevailed since the 1990s, for the far right these are read as symptoms of an ascendant resistance movement against an impending 'replacement' of the 'truly'

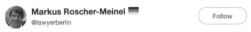

Markus Roscher-Meinel 🏴
@lawyerberlin

`Follow`

Asylanträge von Patrioten aus dem Kalifat werden bevorzugt behandelt. 😉 #Ironie #Scherz #eigentlichtraurig #Deutschland #TDE2017 #Feiertag

12:28 PM - 3 Oct 2017

Figure 2.4 Kalifat Deutschland.

German people. As we have shown, there is no such thing as *Dunkeldeutschland* or an inherent Eastern German resistance. It should be clear that these narratives are made, and that each of these narratives serves political purposes.

The German author İmran Ayata argued that

Right-wing violence and racism are neither exclusive problems of Eastern Germany nor Saxony. Of course, we also encounter group-related hatred from Schleswig-Holstein to Baden-Württemberg, in Europe and on other continents. Having said that, racial exclusion and violence are much older than the reunited Germany. To put it simply, racism is a universal phenomenon that unfolds social realities on the ground and spreads from there via social media at lightning speed. It can therefore no longer be localised. As specific as the social structures and economic and social conditions in Saxony are, racism has little to do with the Saxon mentality. Racism is a dynamic field in which political ideologies, social-psychological attitudes, apparatuses, actors and milieux, social and political contexts and public discourses come together. It is subject to economic cycles and struggles.[82]

Similarly, the Eastern German researcher Matthias Quent argues that racism is not an exclusive problem of Eastern Germany, and people do not become AfD supporters simply because of their experiences with the former GDR.[83] Localising the rise of the right exclusively in Eastern Germany, and asking again and again for the reasons why the East is supposedly more susceptible to extremism, distort the way we think about the East and the way we are researching the far right. But 'Germany is in Saxony,' as Ayata argued: 'What happens here concerns us all.'[84]

3

Renaturing and the politics of *Heimat*

When people hear the [Nazi nationalist slogan] 'blood and soil,' they think of the blood, but the soil part mattered.
Heidi Beirich, intelligence project director
at the Southern Poverty Law Center[1]

Real Germans and the call to repopulate the East

Since 2000, wolves have found new territories in the former East Germany to live and reproduce. The region of Lusatia, a former mining site for coal (with a few mining sites still active today), has particularly benefited from renaturation programmes of the federal government since the early 1990s. According to the Annual Report of the Federal Government on the Status of German Unity 2018, the remediation of areas of the former lignite open mines and the determination of 'a total of 24,700 ha of agricultural and forestry land for a broad variety of nature conservation purposes'[2] has resulted in the renaturing of the landscape, the emergence of lakes and large-scale reforestation, and in these wildlife sanctuaries wolves, wildcats, golden jackals, lynx and a few European bison, among other species, have found a new home.

While these deindustrialisation and renaturation processes contribute to making the East uninhabitable for some – who are not finding jobs, for instance, or medical care, or public transport – others seek to repopulate and reinvent these territories as their new *Heimat*. Nationalists, conspiracy theorists worrying about the Islamisation of (Western) Germany, and esoteric eccentrics are calling for like-minded people to move to Eastern lands.

Amongst these calls to move East we can find small esoteric movements that share the ideals of blood and soil. For instance, the Russian Anastasia movement and so-called *völkisch* settlers have found cheap homesteads, farms and land, far from prying eyes. Far-right splinter parties, such as Der III. Weg, which were banned for their insurrectionist politics in Bavaria, have moved across the border to Saxony. Eastern Germany is thus becoming a haven for outcasts from all over the Republic. This is helped by the call for a new, positive and 'luminous' identity for Eastern Germany that we discussed in the second chapter.

When we talked about the 'glorious' East with a very well-known right-wing activist, then known as a spokesman of the neo-fascist (now defunct and prohibited) organisation THÜGIDA[3] in the autumn of 2018, we came to understand the implications of this framing of 'dark Germany' as particularly luminous. We met Michael Schneider* in the centre of Leipzig, where, looking derogatively at the people shopping at lunchtime, he commented: 'In many ways, this is not my *Volk* any more. I would rather withdraw into my garden or the forest – like a recluse.' But this retreat is no mere private retreat from modernity. Retreating to rural areas is part of a strategy for the far right, as he explained the broader picture:

The goal, of course, is a *reconquista*, a return to our values and what we imagine. But the reality ... I see the Western German states [...] as lost because the population has reached a tipping point in terms of migration. What I see in the near future is a Germany or a country that has been described by George Orwell in his novel *Nineteen Eighty-Four*, this is what we're moving towards. You can extract yourself from this, which is what young people should do, those who are not just submitting to the regime. You should be independent as much as possible, retreating to the countryside and living according to your own thinking and with your families and loved ones.[4]

The advice to retreat to rural areas in the East is related to the far-right master narratives of the 'great replacement' and of resistance (cf. Chapter 2). And the politics of *Heimat* and the politics of renaturing are intertwined with former national socialist and current far-right views on natural habitats for the German ethnos and the German flora and fauna:

the community's natural environment does not just provide resources allowing us to live and prosper, it constitutes an ecosystem: that is, 'the people' (in its territory) is one element of a larger whole. This fundamental interconnectedness of place, plants and non-human animals, and 'the people' requires profound measures to protect the whole and its parts. The elements of such an ecosystem form a symbiotic relationship in which, first, land becomes homeland (Heimat).[5]

This is the ethno-pluralist Blood and Soil hypothesis. In the basic understanding of *Heimat* in far-right ideology, the *Volk* is imagined as a body politic to which individuals are joined by blood and soil. Blood means descent of the peasantry that was allegedly formed by tilling this soil, and thus developed in conjunction with it. The soil is thus not a mere territory but the *Volk*'s natural habitat. The cultural scientist Nils Franke calls this *Geo-determinism*:[6] the land is understood as imprinted on to the physical and psychological attributes of a creature, and this is transmitted to future generations. The right *Volk* living on the right soil is then 'appropriate to the species'. The hard German land thus produces this particular people. The German farmer has produced the German artificial countryside (*Kulturlandschaft*), and, in this view, it is here that the Germans are at home. Industrialisation and, now, globalisation, however, have changed this artificial landscape and alienated the German people from their nature. From this they deduce that a particular *Volk* has a natural title to that land, and others – who do not come from the 'right stock' – do not. In fact, there is an 'appropriate habitat' for them somewhere, or there would be if people had not 'intermingled' and 'degraded' the stock. That is how Jews and Roma are framed: they are thought of as by their very nature non-sedentary peoples who do not belong to any particular soil, as they lack peasant backgrounds, and will thus try to 'intermingle in species' that can become 'contaminated' by them. If a stock becomes contaminated, it induces the end of the species (*Volkstod*). Thus, the far right's move to the countryside is part of an intentional attempt to preserve the German 'species'. The natural order is to maintain the 'species' – as connected to its soil – and, so, true-blood descendants should concentrate in certain areas, according to the far-right narratives: 'The unattractive Central Germany must become a refuge in which depopulation is reversed.'[7]

The reason the *völkisch* settlements are deemed a problem worth noting by NGOs and by journalists such as Andrea Röpke and Andreas Speit is the fear that the settlers may be partly responsible for the move to the right among the general rural population, as a sort of contamination by *völkisch* nationalist thinking carried into the countryside by urban extremists.[8] And indeed, some far-right think-tanks do call for such an undermining of rural milieux: rural regions have the advantage that the local population can be influenced: in theory, if families come with children, these can be sent to the local kindergartens and schools, and their parents can then influence what is being taught through becoming active in the parents' associations and thereby politically and socially influence local society.

In reality, the settlements have not been very successful, even though this is a development thirty years in the making, but they are part of a long-term strategy of white nationalists to infiltrate the countryside and influence everyday culture there. Just as far-right activists have been reported to infiltrate sports clubs to engage in military training, survival training and martial arts sports in order to be able to defend the *Volk* when necessary,[9] there are reports of attempts by right-wing organisations to take over environmental and rural cultural organisations as well.[10] There is a magazine dedicated to right-wing protection of the *Heimat* under the guise of environmental protection: *Umwelt & Aktiv* describes itself (in Bernhard Forchtner's translation) as *Magazine for Holistic Thinking: Environmental Protection – Animal Welfare – Homeland Protection*. In Germany, Forchtner argues, 'environmental concerns and ecological thinking have long been interwoven with *völkisch*, Social Darwinian and racist ideas'.[11] The magazine describes its aim as defending the local against the 'internationalists':

> In our own country, we find ruthless internationalists supported and fawned over by established political parties, especially those who claim to protect the environment and animals. Such so-called global players turn our homeland into a plaything of international financial trading. This

affects everyone, no matter their political disposition. The farmer as a modern self, the consumer as uninformed customer. We want to show you how environmental protection and animal protection serve foreign interests and interested parties which operate in secret to the detriment of our homeland and our people.[12]

Far-right settlers in the rural regions who are engaging in conservation activities are striving for self-sufficiency and in particular, economic independence of modern urban infrastructures. To escape the cities that are, according to this narrative, 'run by internationalists,' or, in the words of THÜGIDA representative Schneider, 'tilted' in terms of the size of their migrant population, the idea of settlement remains a central narrative in far-right strategic thinking against the background of the 'great replacement' conspiracy theory. In *Umwelt & Aktiv* and the New Right magazine *Sezession*, settlement projects have been a recurring topic. The journalists Andrea Röpke and Andreas Speit see the established *völkisch* settlements as potential fortified villages (*Wehrdorf*). These share the characteristics laid out by the National Democrat Steffen Hupka in his 2012 pamphlet *Neue Wege*, who argues that settlements should be founded on the basis of '1. A steadfast national socialist worldview. 2. Unconditional willingness to self-sacrifice unto death. 3. Racial kinship to the Germanic peoples and genetic soundness'; these attributes are supposed to be the preconditions for a new life in absence of everything that makes us ill, towards a 'new, self-determined, good and healthy little world'.[13] Empirical evidence shows that the villages that are called *völkisch* by the journalists are characterised by drinking parties, May dances, festivals of light in the autumn, summer and winter solstice parties and a very conservative dress code, with dresses for women and girls, and carpenters' trousers and white shirts for men. But that is not quite the same as unconditional willingness for self-sacrifice etc. They are mainly ultra-conservative cliques, some of them with indubitably sectarian characteristics.

About a dozen settlements that count as *völkisch* are run in accordance with the esoteric teachings of the Anastasia sect. They consider urban lifestyles to be decadent and degenerate and advocate living in kinship homesteads. The ultimate aim is world peace:

> Each of us should take his own parcel of land and build his small but concrete paradise, with all his brainpower and all his spiritual might. Let us take a lovely spot on this planet and turn it into an everblooming garden and thus manifest our spirituality, as God has done. If millions of people over the world do this, the entire earth will be a blooming garden, and there will be no more wars, because millions of people will be kept busy with a common creation.[14]

These parcels of land are to be managed by a (strictly heterosexually organised) family that is to have its own family compound, to each compound a pond, vegetable patches and fruit trees, as well as a forest in which to bury the dead and in which to remember the ancestors. It is ideally a self-sustaining microcosm. According to the homepage of the Anastasia Foundation, 'The kinship homestead is a parcel of land of not less than one hectare (100 × 100 m) for the permanent residence of one family, where the family can build a house with love, plant a tree, own a forest, a garden, and equip a pond. The kinship homestead is enclosed by a hedge of forest cultures: cedar, coniferous and deciduous trees, shrubs.'[15]

The kinship homestead is ideally surrounded by up to three hundred further kinship homesteads. It is believed that those who come from such a homestead will reincarnate and increase their levels of perfection. The other kinship homesteads might include an ethno-nationalist extension of immediate kinship relations, but this depends on the local forms of the movement, there being no central organisation that deduces political points on the basis of the ten books in which the 'true teachings' of Anastasia are revealed.[16] Some argue that some family backgrounds would be better than others, and the 'Ringing Cedars' Anastasianism argues that Slavic or Russian backgrounds are among the better – they talk not of Aryan stock but of 'Slavic-Aryan Vedas' or 'Brother Peoples'.

The Anastasia settlement movement is a relatively recent development in Germany and hasn't seen much scrutiny by reliable researchers. Only Anna Rosga (2018) interviewed members of the Anastasia movement in three different homesteads for her Bachelor thesis. According to her, they live in timbered mudbrick buildings, tend to have private power generators and biological water purification systems, as well as large vegetable gardens and orchards, the products of which they sell. It seems that they see gardening as producing personal relations between the vegetables and the gardeners, and the vegetables as part of the great circle of life giving back the goodness to the gardeners that they have themselves received from them. As one Anastasia member explained: 'I spend every day on the land, and I truly receive ideas from it that are not my own. They come from the land.' But the plants would also give the believers contact to the ancestors, especially through growing trees, they said. The seed, before it is planted, must be taken into one's mouth in order to imbue it with 'bioenergetic' information. This way, the plant knows the bloodline and help connect planter with their ancestors and alert them to their presence:

We can call to the ancestors, but a human life can be a bit too short for success. That is why we use the plants, as they get a bit older and steadily call out to them and gather the ancestors, the great-grandparents and great-great-grandparents and so on. And they are then present with a share of their souls. And this helps the bloodline to gain strength and they give back, we also gain strength through them.[17]

And this is the reason why, for followers of the Anastasia movement, people should stay in their own lands: their uprooting would weaken their relation to their ancestors and weaken their offspring, and this is to betray the godly being on earth. The movement is against migration, against refugee settlement and in particular against Jews, who are thought to be part of the 'dark powers'. In their thinking, Jews are said to pollute the 'German soul', which would lead to meat consumption and environmental degradation.

The Anastasian settlers claim to be establishing a new order and, in doing this, saving the world by purifying it and providing a new basis for a renewed (kinship-based ethnic) unity – a new beginning for the *Volk*. In many ways, then, such movements have much in common with traditional Nazi blood-and-soil ideologies and its racist assumptions about foreign bodies infiltrating the natural order. The German version of the movement is thus often said to be decidedly right-wing and particularly anti-Semitic. Still, its anti-Semitism is deemed to be harmless by the Federal Office for the Protection of the Constitution[18] and the settlers themselves do not consider themselves right-wing.[19]

The goal of other nationalist settlers (*völkische Siedler*) in building homesteads is based on ideas similar to those of the Anastasia movement, that is, self-sufficiency, one hectare per homeland, kinship living and esoteric beliefs, for instance, in 'awakening Aryan awareness in the tribes' and 'purifying men and land'.[20] One of the websites that propagates these values unabashedly refers to the Nazi think-tank and research institute Ahnenerbe (in English, 'ancestral heritage') that operated in Germany between 1935 and 1945 and was a research institute established by the SS, founded to prove the racial superiority of 'Aryans'. Frank Willy Ludwig, who runs the 'Urahnenerbe' website and offers healing rituals, claims to have had visions of the Anastasia books in a trance, and claims to have his own knowledge about transcendental facts to disseminate. Besides referencing the Anastasia books, Ludwig refers to the neo-pagan Russian polytheistic sect Ynglism with its views of the great white race ('Aryan-Slav') and its variations of Swastikas and the Nazi symbol *Irminsuls*, as well as its use of the raised right arm as a 'traditional' greeting. So esoteric anti-Semitic sectarianism does become fused with traditionally right-wing racism in current political practice.

Whilst there are very few known hamlets of *völkisch* settlers and a handful of members of the Anastasia movement, and whilst their connections to far-right ideologies are under-researched, they do exist. What makes them catch public attention above and beyond their significance in numbers is that right-wing think-tanks are calling for a resettlement of the East. In fact, Höcke has repeatedly talked about the far right's retreat to the 'Gallic villages' in former Eastern Germany, in order to build them as strongholds, repopulate them with 'real Germans' (in an imagined contrast to 'tilted' cities in the former Western Germany) and strike back against the equivalent to the 'fading Roman Empire' which to him is the Federal Republic of Germany.

In his book Höcke suggested in the context of an alleged 'collapse of nation states':

> I mentioned the possible retreat at the Federal state level, for which in particular the East still has great potential to stop the inhumane project that is the migration society. [...] In case of such a retreat, we reserve the strategic option of 'Gallic villages'. When push comes to shove, we will retreat to our rural refuges such as once the courageously light-hearted Gauls. The new Romans who reside in the dilapidated cities will find a hard nut to crack in these Teutonic Asterixes and Obelixes! We Germans – at least those who still want to be German – will then be just another people among others. But the re-tribalisation in the course of the multicultural conversion is a fallback, the embryonic new start of our people. And one day, this fallback will become the position from which we shall sally forth to kick off the reconquista.[21]

For these far-right political agents, 'national rebirth' has a time and a place: it is set in former Eastern Germany. Teleologically, the narrative ends not in the catastrophe of the Germans dying out but in salvation from the brink of catastrophe.

These narratives of 'great replacement', 'national resistance' and 'national rebirth' were not invented by the AfD. In fact, most of these ideas date back to the nineteenth century, and today, with the rise of the right we have been observing on a global scale, these narratives 'have come to dominate the ideology of extreme-right groups, providing the ideological glue which ties together an increasingly cohesive, networked and transnational extreme-right'.[22] This particular local narrative on the East as more genuine and a refuge from the complexities of modern life contributes to the AfD's special appeal in the Eastern states of Germany because it resonates with particular conceptions of 'us' versus 'them', of *Heimat*, of a once successful resistance against a dictatorial regime and with a politics of belonging that is widespread among the rural population.

Balcony environmentalists, hunters and farmers: narratives of *Heimat* in dispute

The return of the right-thinking Germans to the East to repopulate the (imagined) 'empty lands' goes hand in hand with ideas of 'purification' of German territories and strong anti-immigration attitudes. These ideas are neatly interwoven with anti-globalisation, anti-system and anti-cosmopolitan themes, and fuelling attacks of the AfD against the Green party, city dwellers and Western Germans. All these figures operate as imagined enemies. Interestingly, the political debate around the return of the wolves to Germany has produced a similar set of projected enemies. Focusing on these similarities and on how anti-wolf and anti-immigration narratives propagated by far-right agents relate to one another can shed light on what really seems at stake here – that is, how the abstract concepts of a German nation, a German *Volk* and the *Heimat* are thought of, imagined and, ultimately, disputed.

While researching for this book, we talked to different people who were, in some way or another, affected by the wolf issue, among them farmers, hunters, local residents in rural areas and conservationists. These conversations reveal some of the micro-politics that – on the surface at least – relate to the wolf problem, and yet also move beyond it. Wolf politics often serves as an entry point for expressing deep-felt disparagement towards urban dwellers and Western Germans. The former were, by the rural population, thought of as mere 'balcony environmentalists', as a farmer living in the Saxon Ore Mountains explained to us, reproducing in fact a widespread point of view in Eastern rural regions.

Take Frank Michelchen* as an example. Frank Michelchen is a homesteader in the Brandenburg Spree Forest. He was raised on a nationally owned farm in the GDR, studied to become an agricultural engineer and worked for a *Landwirtschaftliche Produktionsgenossenschaft* (LPG, state-run agricultural co-op) for several years until the country came to its end. After the revolution, he set up his own farming business. Today, he owns 100 hectares of land and about fifty cattle, and he described himself in the first few minutes of our interview as Christian, conservative and very attached to his *Heimat*. Recently he became engaged in politics, although he explained he never intended to ('My father was the mayor for thirty-five years,' he explained, 'and I always thought it to be an invidious job and I said to myself, this is not for me').[23] Only after several of his calves were attacked by wolves, he founded the initiative 'Wolf-free zones' with the help of the local farmers' association. He explained the reason for his political activity: 'Because we are being ruled by people who live in cities, because that's where the majority of the population live, they and their perceptions determine the outcome of elections – not these few poor country folk.' Principally he feels that the city people are making decisions that affect agriculturalists. He and his colleagues use the term 'obnoxiousness' to describe current wolf politics. According to him, wolf protection policies are ruining the traditional rural lifestyle.

> I was raised outside. After breakfast I was gone, and only came back for lunch. We went into the woods to play, we did this and that. And today, young parents with their small children or with grandmothers no longer go into the

woods to forage for mushrooms, just because they're afraid, because the wolves are drawing close to the villages. Just last week, the wolves came to Schönwalde and attacked sheep in the village. Many find this intolerable. So, what am I supposed to do? It doesn't work the way it is; it just doesn't work for us. You're destroying rural ways of life. And that is all we have, our freedom and our values.

The farmer supports a regulation of the wolf population – a euphemism for killing wolves – in order to maintain the free and unfettered lifestyle which he remembers from his childhood. He singles out the Green Party as allegedly dictating his way of life: 'They want to dictate how we are supposed to be living in the countryside.' The Greens do this by propagating a politics of fear, dramatising climate change and putting people in a state of hysteria, he argues:

> Yeah, we all are going to die, either because of the climate or nitrogen oxide or carbon dioxide, we can't decide yet, but it [the catastrophe] will come. And I must say, when I look at the lifestyle of those who vote for the Greens, living in the cities, I might tend to agree. When I look at them, in the big cities in concrete and asphalt and their consumption and nobody thinking about the next day, I probably would have a bad conscience myself.

Michelchen has been farming organically since the early 1990s – not because of political incentives or decisions but because he regarded 'sustainability' as the cornerstone of rural living: 'It actually is a typical way of thinking for farmers, I'd say, we think in generations. A shareholder thinks in quarterly numbers, and we are thinking in generations.' The problem he sees with current policies is that they are hypocritical and ultimately unsustainable, and they dump the responsibility for climate change on farmers without really carrying any of its costs. And so he has come to see the AfD as the least evil in the current party landscape. 'Especially in

Eastern Germany, I think, the AfD is so successful, because of their big mouths, and even if they don't really have that many solutions, they at least tackle the problems people are worrying about.' Previously, he had always voted for the CDU. To him the AfD is 'neither able to rule nor do they have good concepts, but they are resonating with people's feelings – I have said it a few times already: I have the same feeling I had in 1985, 1986, and we all had that feeling, that the system is going down the drain – that nothing works any more.'

As Michelchen explains, people vote for the AfD not because it supports right-wing politics but rather because it is the least of all evils: he says the other conservative parties are spineless, the Greens and the left cater to the urban classes only, and, even if the AfD has no real solutions, its electoral success leads to a soul-searching amongst the mainstream parties. The future might be bleak, in the short term, and a political catastrophe inevitable, but, as he sees it, it is the urban classes who will run into trouble, the farmers being most resilient to this sort of social upheaval. For they can just take the law into their own hands:

> The farmers finish off [the wolves] with poison, but if the state does not convey to the people that it protects them and cares for them, and then you slip into anarchy. And that is the worst-case scenario. But due to this constant political dawdling, it is increasingly likely that something will happen. And when I look at how interlinked all this is, all the nepotism and the racketeering, you really don't want to look behind those curtains. This is something that I am seriously worried about. But my grandfather always told us: 'Child, we are farmers, we will neither starve nor freeze.' The basic needs, a roof over my head, a warm home and eating my fill, that I got covered. And now I tell my son, we here in the countryside can cope with any crisis, we will come off just fine. It will hit the people in the cities rather badly though.

Rural resentment against urban politicians does go some way to explain the rise of the right in Europe and the United States. Katherine Cramer has shown this for Wisconsin. These divides between urban and rural populations, Cramer explains, do not just reflect political disagreements but quite fundamentally reveal people's 'ideas about who gets what, who has power, what people are like, and who is to blame'.[24] As the farmer puts it, 'They want to dictate how we are supposed to live.'[25] Cramer calls this form of thinking 'rural consciousness', defined as

> an identity as a rural person that includes much more than an attachment to place. It includes a sense that decision makers routinely ignore rural places and fail to give rural communities their fair share of resources, as well as a sense that rural folks are fundamentally different from urbanites in terms of lifestyles, values, and work ethic. Rural consciousness signals an identification with rural people and rural places and denotes a multifaceted resentment against cities.[26]

Knowing this, it becomes clearer why the AfD is strategically targeting rural regions in Eastern Germany in its campaigning efforts. The AfD successfully taps into widespread rural resentments against city folk, amplifying them and making them productive for their purposes of gaining people's votes. In one of the AfD campaign events in Grosspösna, a small town in Saxony, in March 2019, the local AfD representative Jörg Dornau explained that he focused on rural regions, that he is himself a farmer and that farmers should be supported and rural regions should be preserved: 'This is our land, this is our *Heimat*,' he explained, 'and we will protect and preserve it.'

But what, or whom, does this land need to be protected from? Local hunter Thomas Frieder*, a resident of Leipzig, talked to us in his game-processing shed while he was gutting a fresh deer carcass. The way he saw it, the natural world he lives in needs to be protected from wolves. He sees wolves as an invasive species with no right to exist on his hunting grounds. 'Right now, the wolf can spread as freely as it wants, it is welcomed everywhere, without considering the effects on the established age-old culture, which is left to adjust to the recently immigrated wolf.'[27] He sees the balance of the whole ecosystem as imperilled. In the end, drinking a *Schnaps* to the deer he was eviscerating, he argued that hunters will eventually be taking the matter into their own hands: 'We have a system: three S – shoot, shovel, and shut up,' he laughed, meaning that hunters illegally shoot the wolves and bury them deeply in the woods. In the hunter's view this is justified as an act of resistance.

The hunting ban on wolves is basically illegitimate, he argues: 'In essence, the conservationists are in the minority, and they benefit from lobbying, politics and the media, but it is important that we accept that minorities are not supposed to oppress the majority, and that the minority cannot force its opinion upon the majority.' He feels patronised when it comes to wolf politics.

> What do I wish for in society? Reason and experience should make a comeback. Nobody should point a finger at us and say: 'He murdered a deer!' [...] In particular, this aggressive way in which vegans deal with meat-eaters, this is one-sided. And in our society, it is conspicuous how our democracy has changed, that minorities are dictating to the majority. [...] For example, if the majority are driving a car and the majority are doing that because they need to or want to, then the minority has to just put up with that.

The wolf here stands not just for a predatory animal but for an occasion for urban dwellers to patronise, belittle and pick on hunters and other 'good country folk'. In these anti-urban narratives, townsfolk mutate into judgemental vegans, bossy cyclists, and minoritarian dictators. The AfD's complaints against an alleged current dictatorship are perhaps not so much to be taken literally – in contrast to the two twentieth-century German dictatorships, there are no prison, labour or genocidal camps, no political prisons, no persecution for having the wrong opinions. But they problematise the widespread moralising about environmental issues and climate change concerns. It is thus perhaps not so much the government that the rebellion is against as it is against the *Zeitgeist*, which appears to dictate a way of life that is best called *transnational*. Transnational politics no longer takes place within the territory of the nation but finds itself formed through social contexts that transcend individual states' territories.[28] Wolf politics are EU politics; refugee management is based on the Dublin rules, again an EU policy; the political reactions to climate change are global. And what these transnational 'townies' are perpetuating is seen as a 'culture of condescension'.

This 'culture of condescension' by a 'minoritarian dictatorship' is ruining the system of power hitherto known as democracy, from this perspective. Minorities are governing 'the majority', townies dictating to 'real people', Greens are telling 'us' what to eat: 'we' are infantilised, the new right wing argues, and 'we' are having none of it. Furthermore, these minorities are trying to decide who gets to live here, migrants, wolves, what else? Our hunter believes in the inherent right of certain species to live in certain territories, and only these species are to have this territorial right. As he see it, all other species, all newcomers, are no better than invaders.

In this perspective, both wolves and newly arriving humans then need to be regulated, otherwise the habitat would reach a natural tipping point: disaster looms. Ironically, for the hunter, those who call themselves and their politics 'green' are at the origin of the impending devastation. Unless, that is, 'we' engage in conservation properly. Keep out the wolves, keep out the migrants, and preserve the local ways of life, for the deer, our women and our children. After the Second World War, the hunter explains, Germany flourished precisely because of the decimated population. The numbers have risen again, war or worse might very well loom. 'Sickness, epidemics, war, emigration – somehow, the population will be regulated and if you want to harm a country, you'll allow immigration. [...] If you let people immigrate into a country, you increase the population density, increase the conflicts, and at some point, the problems,' the hunter explained. Talking about *Heimat* is, then, a way of talking about who or what belongs here and who does not. Here, Germany is thought of as a functioning ecosystem that needs to be protected from invaders and from external threats. In the hunter's line of thought, 'indigenous' species have the right to regulate 'invasive' ones.

In contrast, conservationists like Stephan Kaasche from the Contact Office Wolves in Saxony (Kontaktbüro Wölfe in Sachsen) argue that 'new' and 'old' populations need to adapt to each other. For Stephan Kaasche, the returning wolves had already adapted to artificial landscapes in Poland or the Baltic countries (where they had come from), and the wolf therefore does not particularly need to adapt to being in Germany, on the contrary, humans had to adapt to the wolves' presence. More importantly, the wolves are useful as scapegoats for a number of structural issues, as he saw it:

> I was giving a talk about wolves, and one man in the audience said: 'You cannot keep sheep any more!', and another man said: 'The people here are so poor, they need to have

livestock in order to provide meat for themselves.' His theory was that the wolves had been imported in order to kill all the livestock, so that the people were forced to buy their meat from the supermarkets and throw even more money at the big corporations. I said to the man: 'Okay, but if you shoot all the wolves, would people be rich again?' In other words, he did recognise poverty among the elderly as a structural problem, but, logically, shooting wolves is not a solution to that problem. What would help are minimum pension payments, local job opportunities, that the children don't emigrate, so that they are not alone when they're old ... that would help more than shooting wolves. Shooting wolves won't solve any real problem.[29]

The wolf-affected regions, particularly in the East, are regions rife with structural problems. But as all political utterances coming from the East are discredited as right-wing, wrong-headed, ungrateful and ignorant, there is no way of articulating these demands successfully, so it seems. People complain about wolves, they are always heard when they talk about wolves. And so the wolf becomes a scapegoat.

Furthermore, the wolf operates as a figure with which different narratives are being (re-)produced and disputed. First, the figure of the wolf is a protagonist in the politics of fear that helps far-right populist parties such as the AfD appear as a party that cares for the needs and worries of the rural population, while simultaneously tapping into widespread anti-immigration, anti-urban and anti-government resentments. Second, the wolf tends to be conflated with particular conceptions of *Heimat*, whereby elements of the far-right blood-and-soil ideology seem to thrive. Third, with the help of the wolf, different conceptions of invasive species and alien populations are being expressed, while the value of *Heimat* landscapes and territories is being elevated.

And fourth, the wolf figure assembles an array of conceptions of an alleged invasive and domineering foe, among them Greens, urban dwellers and Western Germans.

Among wolves: *Neue Heimat*

We are witnessing a trend within global far-right movements to rediscover nature and the environment as 'natural' models for the social order: 'nature's laws are not limited to plants and non-human animals',[30] but are equally applied to human populations. These trends are discussed as 'eco-xenophobia', 'eco-fascism', 'eco-naturalism' or 'right-wing ecology' and an equation of conservationism with the protection of the *Volk*.[31] In order for the people to be pure, the soil needs to be kept pure as well and vice versa. Whilst certain minorities were long seen as unsuitable for this soil, it is modernity that comes back as a main problem among the far right. In their perspective, modernity is 'a social order parasitic to the natural world', and which alienates 'consumerist individuals [...] from natural ways of life'.[32]

In February 2017 Jack Donovan travelled to Germany to perform a ritual in a village located in Saxony-Anhalt. Jack Donovan is a protagonist of the white supremacist group Wolves of Vinland that is situated in the US state of Virginia. Wolves of Vinland is a small, tribal-like group of white men who subscribe to a brand of neo-pagan Norse theology.[33] Donovan is connected to the New Right think-tank Institute for State Politics (Institut für Staatspolitik, IfS) led by Götz Kubitschek,[34] and in his blog he presents himself in highly stylised photographs as buff and tattooed, upper body exposed, standing beside bonfires in the woods and holding rituals. Donovan is the author of several books, among them *Becoming a Barbarian, A More Complete Beast* and, most prominently, *The Way of Men*. On the basis of his online and offline writing activities mainly on the topic of masculinity, Donovan can be considered as part of the US far-right 'manosphere', as the author Donna Zuckerberg has termed the online communities of white male supremacists of the Red Pill movement who 'believe they need solidarity with each other because the idea of white male supremacy is an illusion maintained to ensure they remain oppressed'.[35]

Donovan's *The Way of Men* has been published in German translation by Kubitschek's own New Right publishing house Antaios, and in this book Donovan attempts to explain the values of 'primal masculinity'. He explains that 'the Way of Men is the way of that gang'.[36] For Donovan the 'natural' state for men to exist in is the form of wolf packs. Only among wolves can men be who they 'really' are, based on strength and survival skills such as hunting and fighting. Donovan explicitly refers to Thomas Hobbes's idea of the 'natural state of men', which he disagrees with because of the 'nature' of such wolf packs:

> Hobbes' idea of *warre* is interesting on a theoretical level, but this *warre* of all against all is not the state of nature for men. It's natural for a man to look after his own interests, but those interests drive men together – *quickly*. A loner has no one to ask for help, no one to watch his back, no one to guard him when he sleeps. Men have greater chance of survival together than they do apart. Men have always hunted and fought in small teams. The natural state of *warre* is ongoing conflict between small gangs of men.[37]

Thus, it is 'the job of men to draw the perimeter, to establish a safe space, to separate *us* from *them* and create a circle of trust'. This they do by 'gathering together, establishing hierarchies, staking out land and using strength to assert their collective will over nature, women, and other men'.[38] Donovan's thinking and writing are explicitly opposed to 'the system', the government and, most importantly, modern civilisation, which, as we learn from his 2017 speech at Kubitschek's IfS, poses a most 'unnatural order' for men to live in. Men are naturally violent, and

> Those who give names in modern democratic states today obscure that violence. Many in the American law enforcement community have even convinced themselves that they are special sheep dogs who protect good, civilised, modern people – who are theoretically incapable of violence – from anyone designated a 'criminal.' In this bizarre and self-serving delusion, anyone who the state identifies as a 'criminal' is some kind of sick and evil sub-human whose only motivation is to prey on that good, modern, civilised sheep. [...] It's easy to live in a world of lies. [...] When a man allows himself to be convinced that violence is evil, he confines himself to a world as simple and distorted as a child's drawing. He's emasculated, alienated from the morality of the master, and resigned to the sentimentality of the slaves.[39]

The Wolves of Vinland around white supremacist Jack Donovan might be an extreme example, but the similarities of his thinking with, for example, the thinking propagated by Kubitschek's New Right think-tank, and the similarities in using analogies to sheep and wolves in public speeches to, for example, the speeches of the AfD politician Björn Höcke (see Chapter 2), are noteworthy. As the narratives propagated by these far-right agents are deeply intertwined with anti-feminist, anti-system and anti-globalisation ideologies, they all presuppose a particular notion of *Heimat*, that is a sense in which responsible care of the land and clean, tribalistic living are being championed that have long antecedents in the conservative movements of the nineteenth century and reactionary movements in the twentieth century.[40] What is essentially at stake in these narratives is a politics of belonging – of the 'right' people belonging in the 'right' place. The potentially violent and even murderous consequences of these narratives and the politics of 'us' against 'them' they imply have become obvious: Once again, right-wing terror is on the rise in Germany. Attacks such as the 2016 mass shooting in a Munich shopping mall, the knife attack on the politician Henriette Reker in 2015, the murder of Walter Lübcke and the attack on a synagogue in Halle in 2019, and the most recent terror attack in Hanau in February 2020 have left the country reeling. Whilst some observers evaluate these events as 'lone wolf' terrorist attacks',[41] others warn of a more systematic mainstreaming of far-right attitudes and its role in the increasing numbers of terrorist attacks. In the following chapter we discuss state and state-sponsored reactions to these political shifts, affecting policies, civil society and journalism. In particular, we are looking at the governance of right-wing nationalism in a country that is widely thought of as having successfully denazified itself and come to terms with its troubled past.

4

Herding wayward citizens

Coping with the past as a permanent social task is para-
lysing a people. [...] We do not need anything other more
urgently than a remembrance policy change of 180 degrees,
dear friends. We don't need dead rites any longer in this
country.

AfD politician Björn Höcke[1]

'Lone wolves' and abjects to the modern German nation

When one of us gave a talk to three hundred senior citizens who attended seniors' classes at Leipzig University in
November of 2019, the audience question that received the
loudest acclamation by the public was 'Why do we need
elections? I do my job as a farmer, I'm not elected into that
position, I know what needs to be done and I do it, every
day of the week, but the politicians sit around and have
us pick them every four years. Why can't they just get on
with it? Why are they wasting our time?'[2] Such widespread
resentments against the political class go hand in hand
with the rise of the right. They amount to the sort of statement that gets its speaker called 'populist', populism being
a set of diverse opinions that have one thing in common:
a resentment of the 'elite' and an exaltation of 'common

people'.[3] In this view, common people know intuitively what's best, they are uncorrupted by refinement, abstract ideas, urban living and non-traditional gender norms. And they represent the people in that they embody its will; they *are* the *Volk*, or think they are. And such assumptions about the *Volk* as a non-pluralistic entity with a common volition make up the ideologies of the newer nationalist parties across Europe.

For nationalist parties have been gaining ground across Europe, and the AfD is one among many.[4] However, in the German context, this is seen as shocking, much more so than the rise of the Front National (now Rassemblement national) in France or Vlaams Belang in Belgium, Jobbik in Hungary, the Lega Nord (now Lega) in Italy, the Danish People's Party in Denmark or Vox in Spain. In contrast to all these countries, Germany spends millions of Euros every year – over €100 million in 2019[5] – on civic education in order to prevent German nationalism. And until recently the German government has been fairly successful in preventing these sorts of far-right parties gaining ground. It is perhaps because of this interference with civil and political society that, rather than seeing the rise of German nationalist parties as a belated catching up of European neighbours, scholars are struggling to explain the electoral successes of the AfD, and hypotheses range from the electoral base being driven by economic destitution, by psycho-social deficiencies from having been brought up in a dictatorship, to inadequacies of working-class masculinities or the revenge of the rural and the 'left-bchind' – all of which have been falsified.[6] What often remains after all is said and done is that right-wing attitudes and views, especially in regard to immigration, Judaism and Islam, provide an important motivation for people to vote for the AfD.[7]

Still, it's not as simple as saying that it is old-fashioned racism and new forms of anti-Semitism that drives voters, or that it is just a resurgence of old – National Socialist – attitudes, preferences and worldviews. Far-right think-tanks stress that organisations and movements that are labelled right-wing, conservative or nationalist are not in the least part of 'old' National Socialist traditions. Instead, the PEGIDA movements, the AfD, the Identitarian Movement and the far-right think-tank IfS consider themselves to be part of the so-called New Right.[8] In fact, the New Right is not that new, nor are its efforts to distance itself from National Socialism. When the NPD failed to get enough votes to enter the German parliament in 1969, some of its supporters adopted a so-called Third Position in opposition to both communism and capitalism and tried to infiltrate various left-wing and ecological groups. In the German historical context, the strategy of distancing from National Socialism has been a feature of right-wing nationalist movements ever since. For they are operating in a context in which the German government has institutionalised measures to influence civil society by setting a clear line between problematic ('Nazi') German nationalism and acceptable, civilised, German nationalism, as we will show in this chapter. This is a Sisyphean task and requires ever new modes of control, including the *management of hate*.[9]

The first step someone who wants to participate in acceptable nationalism must take is distance themselves from harmful German nationalisms, or, as a stand-in, Nazism. Thus, even supporters of the far right emphatically strive to distance themselves from views considered National Socialist, just as English Defence League supporters distance themselves from racism.[10] For example, when we interviewed two active members of the current far right, Michael Schneider* and Katharina Schulte*, in November 2018,[11] both emphasised that they were 'honourable' people, socially engaged and 'helping the poorest of the poor'. Though Katharina Schulte admitted to being a member of the far-right initiative Homeland Protection Meissen (Heimatschutz Meissen) and the network White Raven Germany (Weisser Rabe Deutschland), she framed those admissions with references to her doing good. Her friend Michael Schneider* conceded that he had been an active member of the (far-right) NPD in the 1990s, and later a spokesman of THÜGIDA,[12] an organisation that is nominally a local variant of PEGIDA but is considered much more extreme by the German Office for the Protection of the Constitution. He too, however, emphasised that he is not a Nazi. He did promote the new organisation A Nation Helps Itself (*Ein Volk hilft sich selbst*). This is in fact a National Socialist slogan featured on the posters of the National Socialist Winter Relief for the German People calling for contribution to charities that offered food, clothing and coal to the needy, as long as they were not Jews, foreigners, Roma or communist, between 1933 and 1945. The newer organisation also collects charitable donations for the needy, provided they are German. Its Facebook page states: 'We assist those fellow countrymen who receive little assistance in times of growing social injustice. In collaboration with our people.' Again, no references are made to ethnicity, or to what it means to be German, but the restrictive policies with regards to potential beneficiaries is implied in 'our people' and 'fellow countrymen'. Both interviewees emphasised their moral qualities with reference to being members of this group, and yet its name and practices have clear Nazi connotations.[13]

They naturally ignore such connotations. The problem from their perspective is that the current government pretends to be conservative, but is, in fact, a new form of socialism and as such, a dictatorship. To both Schulte and Schneider, the problem of this new 'socialist government' is that it is 'overrun by migrants'. Both emphasised, however, that migration is not the issue as such. To them, the real problems lie with the politics of Angela Merkel and her conservative party, with capitalism and the general decline of the welfare state. Beyond left and right, they see that all dissidents are fighting the 'same enemy'. Their organisation Weisser Rabe explicitly seeks allies from the Social Democrats and the trade unions: 'from the National Socialist to the communist, to the peace activist, the Social Democrat, and the member of the Left Party, everybody sits at the same table, members of the AfD, NPD, and all those citizens' initiatives,' Schneider explains. The project is being attacked by the state, in his view. We wonder whether, by 'attack', they mean that the organisation features in a report by the Office for the Protection of the Constitution as a right-wing organisation and Schneider evasively mutters, 'You know, that sort of thing.' Schulte mentions that they had problems with lawyers due to the name Weisser Rabe, which gives Schneider time to reconsider his response. He then adds:

> Right now, we're tuning our activities down a little to avoid being observed by the Office for the Protection of the Constitution. If I scratch the varnish of the system, it's normal that the authorities start observing me. You just need to look at history: It didn't bother the Scholl siblings [resistance fighters during National Socialism, executed by the regime in 1943] that the Gestapo was observing them. They continued to fight, regardless of whether that was considered good or right by the system. You can have different opinions regarding this. The protesters against the GDR regime weren't intimidated by the intelligence service's observation either. They all lacked the spinelessness we see now [in politicians].

The two thus consider themselves resistance fighters, willing to die, they are implying, for justice, freedom and good governance. This time, they argue, the political monstrosities are not targeted at Jews, Roma or Poles. The current regime is waging a war against its own citizens, they say, and it does this by allowing migration, by granting citizenship to aliens and by over the years replacing the German people with others.

And yet, as they see it, not only are they not recognised for being upstanding citizens speaking truth to power, they are chastened for allegedly being Nazis. 'If critique,' Schulte argues, 'is no longer allowed, we'll end up with Stasi methods. I don't want to be back there [in the GDR]; I don't want to be observed or whatever. I just want to be a free-thinking human being.' And Schneider adds not only that both are affected by observation measures but that they don't even have a chance of joining the more respectable political class. The AfD, they were complaining, has 'lists of incompatibility' (*Unvereinbarkeitslisten*) that prevent those with a 'right-wing extremist' background from gaining membership. Schneider complains that the AfD gleefully includes every former CDU politician who applies for membership, 'although these parties are responsible for the current catastrophic state of this country'. In the end Schulte explained that, like everybody else, they did not 'want to be labelled right-wing – because everybody who expresses his needs is beaten down by being called a Nazi – I can understand that. Because what we are expressing has nothing to do with right-wing anything. Nor does it have to do with left-wing anything either. These are just categories.'

Both Schulte and Schneider see themselves as 'lone wolves' in a lonesome fight against systemic injustices, and in doing so are being impeded by the state, government and society. They feel rejected by their own nation. All they are aiming at is restoring the nation to its old glory. They have experienced being observed and arrested and are excluded from any meaningful form of political engagement, they say.

Committed nationalists are feeling rejected by their own nation, which merits an excursion into the politics of nationalism. In his seminal study on German right-wing extremism and its governance, *The Management of Hate*, Nitzan Shoshan has argued that the fight against 'right-wing extremism' is a basic precondition for a reframing of the historically problematic German nation. The term 'right-wing extremism' in this context is a productive term as, first, it produces a constitutive 'outside' to the German nation and homogenises 'the enemy': '[T]otalitarianism was cast as an absolute other through the strict emphasis on and guarantee of all that which it violated, namely, liberal free-doms, human rights, democratic citizenship, the equality of men, and so forth.'[14] Second, 'right-wing extremism' in turn serves to produce a political 'centre' in distancing itself from the embodiment of a problematic German past, because 'the category of (right-wing) extremism grants dom-inant voices a horizon against which to appear as moderate and tolerant, analogous narrative strategies of displacement govern the performance of moderation and the generation of positions from which to enunciate a bigoted politics within the allegedly excluded political extreme'.[15] Third, the term allows for a reconstitution of the German nation, as it ena-bles the formation of a new collective that demarcates itself explicitly from those rejected and condemned 'right-wing extremists'.[16] According to Shoshan, the regulation of 'right-wing' political delinquents – such as the neo-Nazis he has studied in Berlin-Köpenick – would take the form of an affective regime: the management of hate, as he called it,

operates through normalisation and responsibilisation tech-
niques, with the aim of managing the affects of political
delinquents by turning them into self-controlled people:

> temperamental excesses must be inhibited, immoder-
> ate desires reined in, and abnormal demeanors checked.
> Overindulgence in alcohol and unruly violent propensities
> invite corrective interventions that draw on therapeutic
> models to assuage insidious or disgraceful drives. But, as we
> have seen, in Germany, this disciplinary regime links up with
> a web of legal codes, juridical norms, and law enforcement
> procedures that together make up that expansive terrain of
> praxis and knowledge that I have termed the governance of
> hate.[17]

In Germany interventions against right-wing extremist
youth violence and anti-democratic attitudes are organised
mainly in the civil society sector and carried out by non-
profit organisations. State programmes finance projects by a
variety of adult educational institutions, organisations and
associations. Whilst juvenile violence, assault and homicide are prosecuted, 'right-wing extremism' is made to look
like an administrative problem that can be solved by funding enough programmes to combat it. These programmes
also serve to assure the democratic elites: *you are doing
something in the fight against the right.*[18]

Shoshan shows that these state-funded programmes
serve the establishment of Germany as a 'responsible' and
'friendly' nation.[19]

> The fabrication and safeguarding of a healthy, normal nation
> proceeds in and through its inoculation against a sick,
> deviant one. Taken as a set of strategies, discourses, poli-
> cies, institutions, and performances, the suppression of the
> national spectre hence enables the safe return of the nation
> in two crucial senses. First, it mollifies anxieties and mis-
> givings about the menace of latent nationalist undercurrents

by parading as a guarantee against their resurgence and as a pledge of sustained investment in their suppression. But, second, it generates a collective idiom, an institutional architecture, and a set of practices around which a different figure of the national collectivity comes into focus.[20]

In interlocking the civic society and the state, these programmes set a production process in motion, 'in which the tolerant nation is imagined, rehearsed, and performed'.[21] In the end it is all about the rehearsal of moral and nationalist discourses:

All these phrases, and a number of others, too, outline a moral space for the nascent nation and set out some of its key ethical principles. It is to be a nation that places value on its own diversity; condemns monochromatic national imaginaries; respects, accepts, and shows interest in the larger world around it; eagerly fulfils its moral obligations to civility; and stands up to evil. Its national subjects, then, would not only subscribe to cosmopolitan and multicultural values but would also be expected to demonstrate the proper character, to show, in other words, the decency, courage, and commitment to defend those values. Defending those values, each of which – including the very courage to fight for them – clearly references and marks a contrast with the National Socialist past (and, to a lesser extent, the communist one), implies here making both Germany and the world at large safe from German nationalism itself.[22]

The governance of 'right-wing nationalism' in Germany has an institutional setting different from that in most other countries not so focused on their genocides. In Germany the expression of far-right ideologies is censored by state institutions and public opinion. As the historian Mary Fulbrook explains,

For Germans across Germany there is the problem of an inadequately resolved confrontation with the Nazi past. There had been, since the 1950s, various defined, state-ordained positions which one must hold in order to be respectable – for example, in the absence of any real experience of Jews, an attitude of philosemitism – as well as others which were highly sensitive. The issue of national pride was extraordinarily difficult; in 1983, for example, while 92 per cent of Britons were 'proud to be British' and 84 per cent of Italians were proud to be Italian, only 56 per cent of West Germans could agree with a comparable statement about their pride in being German.[23]

After the end of the National Socialist regime, the 'denazification' programme did not actually eradicate anti-Semitism, anti-pluralism and extreme forms of nationalism. After unification the German government funded efforts for civic education in schools, universities and associations of all kinds. Civic education, so the hypothesis goes, could prevent fascism from ever returning to German politics. As the German poet Max Czollek argued recently, these efforts resulted in a particular self-conception of the German people, as it was supposedly proven that the Germans had 'learnt their lesson' and would now be part of a 'new, purified unified Germany [...] immunised against all questions regarding possible continuity'.[24]

Yet these education programmes are increasingly ineffective in some circles. Nationalist, anti-Semitic and chauvinistic tendencies are becoming normal again.[25] Worse, in some regions far-right networks have been established for decades.[26] It is only those who do not live in rural areas in the East who are shocked by the militant racism and violent attacks as in Chemnitz in 2018.[27] Yet, as we argued in the second chapter, the activities of the far right do have a continuity in both Western and Eastern Germany.

In 2018 alone, the police registered 20,431 right-wing criminal offences.[28] Most of these offences are minor as they include misdemeanours, like publicly giving a Hitler salute or showing a swastika. But we have been witnessing an increase in far-right terrorist attacks across Germany for years. Most notably, in 2000, the deadly series of murders by the terrorist group NSU began. Over a period of seven years, the terrorist network murdered ten people, nine of whom because they seemed to them to be migrants. In 2019 the CDU politician Walter Lübcke was shot at his home. The Jewish congregation in Halle celebrating Yom Kippur in 2019 was attacked by Stephan Balliet, who failed to enter the synagogue, but killed two randomly chosen people. We have been witnessing arson attacks against refugee centres, assaults against visible minorities and people wearing yarmulkes, as well as increasing aggressions against trans and queer people throughout the country.

Politicians and journalists continue to describe these attacks as 'singular cases', and the attackers as 'individual offenders' or as 'lone wolves'. Nitzan Shoshan explains that these are not failures as such: the authorities' continuing efforts to locate 'right-wing extremism' on the 'outside' of the German nation have the function of stabilising the image of Germans as having come to terms with 'our' gruesome past, and that 'we' are better now than 'we' used to be, and that anyone who behaves in keeping with Nazi values is not really German, not in the good, new sense. Externalising the threat of the 'far' right in the form of state-funded education programmes has turned a (culturally, socially and politically) heterogeneous field into a constitutive 'outside'. As Shoshan put it, 'the crusade against insidious, illicit nationalism, as an obscene potential that lurks within the most ordinary forms of life, has ingrained itself as the constitutive kernel of a post-reunification national project'.[29]

By default, people like Michael Schneider and Katharina Schulte are excluded from the newly purified version of the

German people. Labelling such people right-wing extremists or Nazis denigrates them.[30] In consequence, people like
Schneider and Schulte, as well as many politicians in the
AfD, see themselves as victims. It helps them to see themselves as warriors, resistance fighters against a totalitarian
regime. In the words of the philosopher Ian Hacking, we are
observing the feedback loop effects that classification processes have on the classified.[31] For those labelled outsiders
end up labelling themselves the same, and this gets turned
into a badge of honour: they are not followers.

Nor are the AfD members and voters. During the AfD
electoral campaigning events we observed in late 2018 and
early 2019, many of those attending feared being labelled
'right-wing' or 'Nazi' in public just because they express
critical opinions about migrants. Many people argue that
there is a distinction between being a right-wing person
and being a normal citizen who happens to have xenophobic attitudes. Engelbert Merz, whom we introduced in the
Introduction and who had been a speaker at the Dresden
PEGIDA marches, stressed that the solution to a multiplicity of political problems is to ask 'the people'. Whilst this
may sound democratic, it wasn't: Merz insists that, in fact,
he *personally* is 'the people', and thus, this being a democracy, *he* is 'the sovereign'. And the sovereign in a democracy
decides on the course of politics. He has to form several
citizens' initiatives to appear legitimate, to avoid the classification of being right-wing or nationalist, categories he
feels have been invented by 'the left' and 'the Greens' to
delegitimise his political views. In promoting the organisation of citizens' initiatives and direct forms of democracy,
he tries to demonstrate the superiority of his own opinions.

It comes as no surprise that the former anthem of the
National Socialist SA, the so-called Assault Song, has

had a revival in recent demonstrations and rallies of the far right across the country. The logic is, if the 'German people' keep being insulted and vilified, then: 'Germany, awake! Awake!' – as the lyrics go. 'Ring the storm until the earth rises/Under the thunder of liberating vengeance!/ Woe to the people that is still dreaming today!/Germany, awake! Awake!' These lines were openly chanted during the Chemnitz racist riots in 2018, and in the demonstrations of Pro Germany in Berlin that we described in Chapter 2.

The current rise of the right in Germany is characterised by various attempts at reinterpretation of the German past, and the questioning of all these state-sponsored efforts of making the Germans a better people. As a recent study has shown in regard to those reinterpretation efforts, 'the stigmatisation of distant past experiences loses its bite and is perceived as an empty ritual' by far-right agents.[32] For decades Germany did not have a far-right party in the national parliament, and scholars thought the institution-alised efforts of coming to terms with the Nazi past would work as a political 'handicap' for far-right political agents.[33] Now, however, the stigma is used as a resource for far-right parties.

'Germany – Never again!'

In Eastern Germany there has been a historically different understanding of the 'problematic' German nation that has led to a greater attention to the governance of problematic 'leftist' nationalisms. In particular, during reunification, a left-wing political movement called the Antideutsche Bewegung (Anti-German Movement) emerged that rejected every form of German nationalism *per se*. For the Antideutsche, the rejection of the nation initially aims at criticising the nation as the dominant instrument for social organisation. From this perspective, the nation is above all an exclusionary project. 'The nation cannot be a genuinely left-wing project, because it always produces exclusion,' explains Claudia Dreichsel*, the editor of a left-wing journal.[34] The nation and nationalism must be overcome. Her colleague adds: 'For me, the slogan "Germany – Never again!" is above all a rejection of Germany as a specific nation and of German history and I read that also in the style of "Fascism – Never again" or "War – Never again."'

The statement 'Germany – Never again!' arose in connection with the development of the anti-national and anti-German movement within the German radical left at the beginning of the 1990s and can be understood as a political reaction to the reunification of Germany. On 12 May 1990 an alliance of left-wing demonstrators in Frankfurt am Main made headlines in national newspapers. According to the political scientist Robert Ogman, this demonstration created a new movement – the anti-German movement – which rejected any form of German nationalism and even the nation state itself. This movement positioned itself against the backdrop of a tightening of asylum law after the fall of the Wall, the growing neo-Nazism and racist motivated acts of violence and pogroms in Rostock, Hoyerswerda and Solingen.[35] At the heart of the anti-German movement was the fight against nationalist and racist violence as well as the question of whether society could be organised by principles other than nationalist ones.

The rejection of the nation as leftist criticism is a specifically German phenomenon. Robert Ogman draws attention to the fact that leftist movements in other countries generally recognise national orders, but advocate, for example, making the existing nation more pluralistic, inclusive and fundamentally more open. It is controversial whether this is actually a left-wing movement, as Isabel Erdem has pointed out: many Antideutsche see National Socialism not so much as an extreme form of a social organisation but as the result of activities by a set of persons whose most important explanatory attribute is their nationality: they were German. And as such, the Holocaust may happen again at any time, as long as Germans continue to exist. Germans are seen as in principle unreformable – which sounds more like the essentialist claim made by traditionally conservative organisations.[36]

The anti-German publicist Thomas Ebermann describes the connection between his own German identity, the specific German history and the resulting political consequences in an interview: 'Here in Germany, in the nation-state Germany, the greatest of crimes against humanity took place, namely the industrial execution of mass murder, I don't want that to happen anywhere again, never again and certainly not in Germany.'[37] To be German, they are arguing, is to be a Nazi. The poet Max Czollek sees Germany as a community of perpetrators and their descendants. Racism, he explains, pervades German history and shapes the political reality then and now.[38] For the anti-German activists we talked to, the history of the German nation, which is rooted in racism, anti-Semitism and nationalism, is closely linked to German identity, which is why complete rejection seems for some to be the only legitimate way of dealing with the German nation. The publicist Thorsten Mense explained to us:

> In any case, I do not use the 'we' in relation to Germany, nevertheless I am part of this German society and, as part of this German society, I think it is incredibly important to point out the continuity, to point out the story time and

again, the context that people do not want to see, and above all, to reveal the involvement of most of the German families in the Holocaust repeatedly, and poke the wound.[39]

In Gera (Thuringia), we met the members of a non-profit association devoted to working through the history of both German dictatorships (*Vergangenheitsbewältigung*). They organise regular tours of a memorial site in the town. When we asked one of the members if she called herself German, thirty-year-old Natalie Schmid* replied, 'I speak the German language. It's my native language. I think that somehow makes me part of a group. But I do not use the term nation. No. [...] For me, the term still has a connotation, a historical connotation that I do not like.' Uwe Reinert*, a man of about sixty, said: 'The term always has a negative connotation. Already as a child, we had the socialist German nation, I grew up there. The other one [Western Germany] was not a nation. The German nation did not exist until 1989. Now, I have this all-German nation, which displeases me, because everyone reinterprets it for themselves. There is no single term. [...] That's why I can say: I'm German, but I like to be nationality-less German.' Julia Koch*, a woman in her mid-thirties, said: 'That's simply because the Germans themselves have huge issues in using terms like *Heimat* and nation.' And Uwe Reinert replied: 'But still, all the countries around us are all proud of their nations. Only we are not. That's absurd. You probably just have to live with this dilemma.'[40]

Confessing to the German national identity includes, at least for the members of the Gera memorial site association, doing memory and history work. Against such a background, many argue that it is not possible to be proud of the German nation – even if this emotional attitude to the

nation in other countries is normal, as one of the interviewees said. However, the normality in dealing with one's own
national identity is always controversial. The anti-national
left's criticism of the nation aims at ensuring that the crimes
of German history can never or should never be normalised.
They are insurmountable and make any positive reference
to German identity impossible. It is a dilemma, as Uwe
Reinert called it, which is sometimes handled with bitter-
ness. For as we have argued, some have no achievements
for which they get recognition. To lose the option of feeling
pride for the nation is to lose the last recourse for pride for
those feeling 'left behind'.

5

Affective politics[1]

It's not just about mere statistics, but about what the citizen
is feeling. Perception is reality. That means what you feel is
reality, too.

AfD MP Georg Pazderski,during a talk show
on the Berlin-Brandenburg public
broadcaster (RBB), September 2016[2]

Wolves and the politics of fear

In 2019 wolves became one of the most important topics
during the local state election campaigns in many rural
areas of three of the Eastern German *Länder*, Saxony,
Thuringia and Brandenburg. Politicians from a wide range
of conservative to nationalist and far-right parties, including the CDU, Free Democratic Party and AfD, campaigned
for a stricter regulation of the wolf population, for 'wolf-free
zones' and the legalisation of wolf hunts. Sometimes vil-
lagers are greeted by the grizzly sight of their livestock's
mauled and bloodied remains, as Stephan Kaasche, who
organised wolf tours in Rietschen (Eastern Saxony), witnessed.[3] This is upsetting and thus suitable material for
political campaigns that focus on fear and the resentment
about being left behind. Silke Grimm, an AfD MP to the

Saxon parliament since 2014, devised a leaflet for the 2019 election campaign using the photograph of a wolf running through a village, past a small teddy lying flat on its back. This was clearly a photomontage and was criticised as stoking irrational fears of the 'big bad wolf', but Silke Grimm – who admits to never having seen a wolf – justifies the use of the montage: 'Wolves need a lot of meat. And a large wolf population needs more meat. And if it is not held in check, wolves will prey on children at some point'[4] (see Figure 5.1). According to the AfD, the numbers of wolves, like the numbers of migrants, need to be regulated: Both are intruders, both endanger 'our women' and 'our children'. The AfD MPs in the federal parliament call wolves 'invaders' in need of a 'cap' – just as the AfD calls for a cap on migration and

Figure 5.1 Silke Grimm (AfD) on election placard: 'Finally regulate wolf populations!'

refugees. The language used for wolves and migrants is similar, and serves to rouse apprehension.

As the phrasing 'our women' shows, those addressed by such campaigns of fear are largely a conservative male and predominantly rural population, comprising farmers, hunters and hamlet residents who are perhaps losing their status, and thus at least have the hope of becoming protectors. They have organised protests and petitions, collected signatures and hold bonfire vigils against wolves. They do not all share the same concerns, but the upshot is that they want to be heard. Smallholders fear for the viability of their flocks. Grandfathers worry about small children waiting for the bus on windswept rural lanes. Farmers want higher compensation for anti-wolf measures such as electrified fences and trained dogs. Hunters worry about the decimation of deer. AfD and right-wing splinter party politicians on the campaign trail are increasingly tapping into these sentiments that are not new as such but have not been taken up by other political parties. As Katherine Cramer has shown, urban dwellers are not only deemed to determine economic and social policy but they are also seen as less deserving, more likely to be beneficiaries of welfare, more likely to be living immorally, more likely to belong to minority groups and are more cherished by the ruling classes.[5] The country dwellers are deemed racist, backward, losers and are sick of not being heard. These resentments are just the same in Saxon wolf country. The wolf has thus come to crystallise rural anger: It is a figure of disenchantment that has very little to do with the wild animal, and much more to do with resenting urban encroachment into rural life. Urban dwellers think of wolves as worth preserving, but ignore, and, worse, do not care, about the detrimental impact of the wolf on the rural way of life.

This holds true as long as this rural way of life is in the Eastern provinces. When a wolf was spotted in the Western German Lower Saxony, the federal government organised hearings on the sustainability of a large wolf population,[6] thereby increasing Eastern German resentment: Eastern German lives are worth less, it seems. And so, since wolves have returned to German territory around the turn of the millennium, 378 wolves have been found dead – mostly killed in car accidents, but forty-six demonstrably beaten to death or shot. As wolf packs expand into new territories towards the north and the north-west, the damage attributed to wolves has also increased. Attacks on livestock are most common where wolves first arrive and where livestock holders have not yet adapted. But the Federal Wolf Documentation and Information Centre has shown that the number of attacks on livestock does not increase linearly with the increase in wolf packs, as Figure 5.2 shows,[7] but, rather, the number of livestock killed increases, even though livestock make up a very low proportion of the wolf diet.

In 2017, 427 cases of livestock killed by wolves were registered. Yet local newspapers report every incident in which livestock has been found dead – including deaths caused by stray or straying dogs, accidents, unsupervised cattle stillbirths or villainous humans as potential wolf massacres. The *Western Journal* in Lower Saxony claimed in May 2018 that horses had been hunted to death by wolves, a claim disputed by the horse owners. The breeders said that they had no land in the area of the alleged attack, that the entire report was unsubstantiated: no land, no dead horses, no wolf attacks.[8] The most important German tabloid, *BILD*, frequently reports such unsubstantiated attacks, making sure to use question marks. 'Two children injured by wolves?'

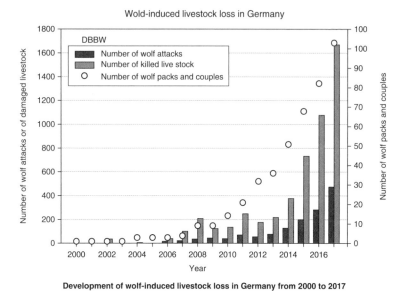

Development of wolf-induced livestock loss in Germany from 2000 to 2017
The year 2000 is the first year of breeding wolf packs in Germany.

Figure 5.2 Wolf-induced livestock loss in Germany.

and 'Shoot the problem wolves!' are two of the numerous headlines related to wolf hysteria in the newspaper *BILD*.

One might surmise that public education might solve the issue, that in fact there have been no wolf attacks against humans for centuries on German territory. But the 'wolf problem' cannot be read in the statistics or the documentation provided by wolf monitoring centres. Conditioned by imagined realities, the core of the wolf problem is a composition of fear and outrage. The wolf is an object of fear, and objects of fear are not only the products of fantasy but an important and effective driving force in politics. The promotion and mobilisation of fear has an old tradition in German politics: the nuclear weapons build-up during the Cold War, the forest decline and the Chernobyl disaster in the 1980s (both of which caused the meteoric rise of the

Green Party), the population census of 1983 and the technical dangers feared before the turn of the millennium. All were met by collective fears to an extent that international observers coined the term 'German angst' as a characterisation of the German national character.

On the occasion of the celebrations surrounding the German unification in 1990, the UK prime minister Margaret Thatcher met with six academic experts on German politics and history to discuss 'the Germans themselves and their characteristics'; in the memorandum, the prime minister's private secretary at the time, Charles Powell, wrote:

> Like other nations, [the Germans] had certain characteristics, which you could identify from the past and expect to find in the future. It was easier – and more pertinent to the present discussion – to think of the less happy ones: their insensitivity to the feelings of others (most noticeable in their behaviour over the Polish border), their obsession with themselves, a strong inclination to self-pity, and a longing to be liked. Some even less flattering attributes were also mentioned as an abiding part of the German character: in alphabetical order, *angst*, aggressiveness, assertiveness, bullying, egoism, inferiority complex, sentimentality.[9]

'German angst' was in fact an invention of English and French politicians and journalists in the 1980s, showing that the seemingly particular German fears have always been a product of media-related dramatisation and political mobilisation. Fears related to war, external enemies, the disruption of the social order, an economic collapse, or apocalyptic threats have successfully been used for political projects throughout German postwar history.[10]

In the current politics of fear, the wolf is presented either as an external enemy or as a disruptor of the social order – as is the immigrant. For the AfD and other small right-wing parties, both wolves and immigrants are figurations

of cross-border migration, cultural strangeness, hybrid identities and transnational interdependences. These figures of
foreignness and invasion crystallise the widespread feelings that the state 'lost control' in 2015 during the summer
of migration, as it did earlier when the wolves came back.
What is more, those who allegedly did not try to 'regain
control' – the Merkel government, in particular, but also
the local Saxon government – are depicted by the AfD as
traitors to the national project, as they broke the covenant
between the state and its loyal subjects that causes the latter
to pledge loyalty in return for sovereignty and safety. The
wolves and the migrants thus stand for a break in the covenant between state and subjects, and the vilification of the
presence of wolves, and migrants, serves to justify a politics
of resistance, a politics that justifies breaking the boundaries
of civility, by (as we have seen in Chapter 2) engaging in
insurrectionist and terrorist violence as well as in discourses
of manifest racism, Islamophobia and anti-Semitism.

The discourses of fear are thus functional: they justify
insurrection and racism; they legitimate the breaking of
the boundaries of civility. As Sara Ahmed has argued, discourses of fear are a central element in nationalist politics
because of the ways in which fear operates in establishing
collectives. She argued that, 'rather than fear being a tool
or a symptom, I want to suggest that the language of fear
involves the intensification of "threats", which works to
create a distinction between those who are "under threat"
and those who threaten. Fear is an effect of this process,
rather than its origin.'[11]

Emotions, according to Ahmed, are psychological states
but they are also practices that 'circulate between bodies'.[12]
Through the circulation of affects, Ahmed argued, social
objects are constituted. No object is inherently worthy of

someone's compassion, and no object is innately conducive to fear. Rather, a social object has to be made that way. According to her, affects are not private properties of individuals but 'play a crucial role in the "surfacing" of individual and collective bodies'.[13] That is, affects form connections between different elements 'by sticking figures together'.[14] In this understanding, wolves are not a threat initially, but the politics of fear invested in the 'wolf problem' is a product of the properties and political functions of fear, or in the words of Sara Ahmed: its circulation and its 'stickiness'.

Affective politics of the German far right and its underlying narratives

Thus, affects are not a natural response to obvious threats, but are politically and socially manufactured. In particular, the politics of fear is an effective constituent of political realities. Many parties mobilise fear to induce political action, and at the moment the Green party and the AfD are the most effective in doing this. Yet neither of these parties would admit that its politics is a politics of fear. In fact, accusing opponents of engaging in a 'politics of fear' is denigrating. Liberals accuse the AfD of mobilising fears, the AfD and other far-right agents bash Green politics for stirring apocalyptic fears of climate change. In one of the German far-right's 'alternative media' blogs, *Völkischer Aufklärer*, current Green party politics are portrayed as fear-mongers:

> The Greens, however, paint a gloomy picture. An apocalyptic picture. Of a perishing and dying earth. This is addressed in particular to young people and families with children. Some are afraid for their own lives, others for the future and the lives of their children. But the green

policy of the Greens is a stun grenade, an incessantly firing *Nebelwerfer* [a Second World War German rocket launcher]. They are not concerned with the future worth living in for the little German girl with plaits. No, at most they are concerned about the future of an oriental girl with a headscarf. So that she can live well in this country. For them, it was, is and will be about one thing only. To abolish everything German. The great German culture, German history, the German nation, and ultimately, the German people.[15]

The far-right author of this blog post blames the Greens for caring about the wrong kind of people and for stirring up the wrong kind of irrational fears. Many AfD politicians, too, have accused the Greens of churning up 'climate hysteria' and for being 'alarmist'. This kind of discourse is intended to vilify the Greens.[16]

The far right is frequently presented as engaging in overly affective politics by harnessing and amplifying a multiplicity of negative emotions. Far-right politics is said to be characterised by the use of fear,[17] the rhetorics of rage and anger,[18] and expressions of hatred.[19] Yet a few problems arise from a dualistic and normative conception of the political affects on the far right.[20] Whilst negative emotions are considered only in the context of far-right politics, more positive emotions are thought to guide more reasonable politics.[21] However, as Sianne Ngai has argued, negative emotions 'are mobilized as easily by the political right as by the left, as the histories of disgust and paranoia illustrate so well'.[22] Furthermore, if we locate negative political emotions at the periphery of politics – that is, the far right – we are adopting a rather comforting perspective that the racist and nationalist political activities associated with the politics of fear, rage and hatred are exclusive features of the political margins, and not the mainstream.[23]

Michael Billig has argued, for example, that, whilst 'nationalism is expected to deal with [...] dangerous and powerful passions', it 'cannot be confined to the peripheries'.[24] On the one hand, negative emotions are not exclusively mobilised by racist and nationalist political agents, and negative emotions cannot be confined to the political fringes of far-right politics.[25] On the other hand, there is more to learn about the role of affects in politics, and 'like other forms of politics, backlash politics are likely to be characterized by more complex and dynamic emotional cultures'[26] than just 'dangerous and powerful passions'.

The idea that negative emotions are a threat to the democratic process is tied to the normative philosophical tradition that considers 'good' politics to be guided by rationality and freed of emotions or the 'passions', to use the Stoic term. In liberal political philosophy, democratic politics have been construed normatively as purely rational.[27] In this line of thinking, emotions are not a conceptual part of politics, and negative emotions in particular are potentially considered a threat to democracy. Against this background, ascribing affectivity to the conduct of a political adversary can operate as a mode of devaluation and delegitimisation.[28]

As we have shown, German populist politicians themselves have embraced and stressed the significance of political affects as something *positive*. The AfD MP Marc Jongen, for example, diagnosed a lack of 'thymotic energy', that is a lack of rage and anger, in Germany's political landscape.[29] Expressing their fears and worries, far-right protesters in Dresden, Chemnitz or Köthen in 2018 represented themselves not as *Wutbürger* but as *besorgte Bürger* ('concerned citizens'). It has been argued that the performance as 'concerned citizens' – as driven by concern rather than rage or anger – would allow far-right agents to present themselves as democratic, resistant and enlightened.[30] In this regard it is made apparent that political affects can have an empowering function, while at the same time both the devaluation of affect and the dualism of truth and affect are being challenged.[31] When the AfD politician Georg Pazderski said in an election campaign in 2016, 'Perception is reality. That means that what you feel is reality, too,' he argued for the truthfulness of emotions, yet in his statement the ambivalence of affect in contemporary politics becomes manifest.[32]

Regardless of the normative dimensions of emotions in political arenas, however, fear is integral to political projects, and further, objects of fear are always entangled in narratives. Yet it seems more interesting to explore the narratives in which these fears are embedded. The far right in Germany, including the AfD, operates with narratives of crisis and threat that structure the political realities of these agents. They frame their narrative, however, as motivated not by fear but by resistance.[33] In one of our interviews with the representative of the far-right organisation THÜGIDA, Michael Schneider*, whom we met in the previous chapter, tried to explain that the categorisations left and right are not useful; what matters to him is who is 'system-obedient' and who performs resistance. Schneider criticises far-right AfD politicians such as Björn Höcke and the founder of PEGIDA, Lutz Bachmann, as 'spineless'. 'brainwashed', 'characterless' and 'submissive' – to him they are political enemies, just like the majority of Germans who, in his eyes, are 'sleeping sheep' who need to wake up and see what is really going on. To him, as to many other members of German far-right groups, it is the German government (the 'system') that is to blame for the cultural and/or civil war that is already allegedly happening in Germany. Without resistance, Germany is about to be repopulated by foreign-ers (*Umvolkung*), leading in the near future to *Volkstod* – the death of the German people.[34]

These apocalyptic and conspiratorial visions are at the heart of the resistance narrative. They are gaining currency in European far-right and populist politics.[35] Because of the allegedly imminent *Umvolkung*, performing resistance and staging a revolution become urgently necessary.[36] The idea of an impending 'great replacement' goes back to the French writer Renaud Camus and is used by Generation Identity activists, eco-fascists, white nationalists and far-right ter-rorists alike. The point is this: fewer than 10 per cent of the German population are actual non-nationals, and 21 per cent of the permanent population in 2015 (before the migration from Syria) have a 'migrant background', that is, at least one of their parents have or have had a overseas citizenship at birth. But among school-age children these numbers are significantly higher, and this is what moti-vates the talk of 'the great replacement': many government agencies point out that migration is necessary and desir-able, given the ageing German population. Some parts of the population deduce that they are to be eliminated, and some use this occasion to reintroduce old representations of transnational Jews determining the fate of the locals.

In these narratives, part of the physical replacement of Muslim bodies for Christian bodies is the war that young Muslim men are waging against 'our women' and in the inner cities throughout Western Europe. Europe, they argue, is in the midst of a civil war, and the liberal governments of the European states are intentionally refusing to protect their citizens from an 'invasion' of Muslims (leading to the 'Islamisation of Europe' of the name of the PEGIDA move-ments). This is because the governments have allegedly been bought by nefarious forces. And the people – those people who vote Green, for instance – are not seeing what is *really* happening, thus leaving the tasks of an insurrection to those who are 'woke'.

In order to explain the recent rise of the right in the Global North from Chemnitz to Charlottesville, we must look into the narratives and affects – and how these narratives and affects are intertwined – of these self-proclaimed resistance movements of the far right. The psychologist Jerome Bruner defines narratives as 'a version of reality whose acceptability is governed by convention and "narrative necessity" rather than by empirical verification and logical requiredness'.[37] As narratives are significant for building and organising realities, they help to provide a frame for social action. In case of the German far right, the resistance narrative is a central driver for collective action and for stimulating a sense of community and solidarity among people who do not have that much in common *per se*, while the outcome of that social action in turn is – as we have witnessed in the Chemnitz riots – powerful affective expressions of rage and hatred.

The narrative of resistance against the great replacement has effects on the organisation of the German far right, too. As we have seen in Chapter 3, in Brandenburg and Mecklenburg-Vorpommern there is a rise of settlements that call themselves ethnically pure, among them esoteric fascists such as the Anastasia movement, the blood-and-soil *völkisch* movements like the Neo-Artaman league, and the neo-pagan and neo-Nazi Artgemeinschaft Germanic Faith Community. Furthermore, some of the so-called *Reichsbürger* ('Reich Citizens') propagate secession from the state in response to the *Umvolkung*.

The invocation of the returning wolf as an object of fear in far-right politics is thus a powerful strategy. Mythologically, the arrival of wolves has always served as metaphor for impending doom, infiltrating evil and existential threats.[38] Thomas Hobbes famously argued that man himself is wolf to man (*homo homini lupus*), unless civilisation intervenes. The wolf, then, is part and parcel of a dualism between good and evil nature, between order and chaos, civilisation and barbarism – and a metaphor for the damage that people do to each other. In refusing to side with civilised man, Hobbes's wolf man has free range to endanger us all. He comes from the wild side within us. To resist the wolf or wolfman is to resist returning to the state of nature. So even though, in a literal sense, the wolf is no threat other than to sheep or deer, as an anthropomorphous object the wolf becomes accessible to political discourse.

The wolf is thus not a political cipher that harnesses fear and resentments as such, yet, when figuring in far-right discourses, it takes on a range of meanings that relate to doom, annihilation, death and destruction. It is therefore not the wolf that is like the migrant but the migrant who takes on meanings similar to the cipher of the wolf.[39] In far-right politics the wolf serves as a figure to construe a (predominantly) rural population as vulnerable to infiltrating populations of predators who have been invited in by urban dwellers who remain luxuriously far removed from the consequences of their decisions. What is at stake, then, is a feeling of solidarity which the far right is seeing as being extended to migrants and refugees, but not to them, not to the poor, not to the conservative and those living rural or small-town lifestyles.

Feeling rules and racist normalities

Late in 2018 we met with four members of a local AfD party in Limbach-Oberfrohna, a Saxon town of about 25,000 inhabitants near Chemnitz, to talk about what it means to them to 'be German', and how they understand the dimensions of German national identity. Quickly the discussion turns towards those who, in their perspective, do not belong. In order to become German, the AfD member Rainer Peters*[40] expects newcomers – 'migrants, refugees' – to behave in a certain way. He explains: 'In my opinion, it is very simple to see who really needs our protection and who just wants to access our social security funds: namely gratitude. If I'm grateful to be here, I'll receive everything with grace, and I'll take what I'm given.' Rainer Peters expects newcomers to be grateful and humble, appreciating the locals' generosity for taking them in.[41] Generosity and gratitude link two groups: 'us' as gracious givers and 'them' as grateful recipients. To expect gratitude is a civilised way to perform a sense of moral superiority that comes, at a closer look, with German national identity.[42] Of course, this expectation is frequently frustrated, as we often heard. Newcomers are tired, bored and anxious, overwhelmed by bureaucratic requirements, foreign foods and baffling expectations, and have not asked for or want the used bikes or the used clothes of the locals. Their destitution is not so absolute that they are happy with undignified scraps. The locals, having experienced indigence a few decades previously, want to be the ones to whom, finally, others might finally be grateful, but this hope is thwarted, and what sticks is that the refugees are unappreciative, graceless, ingrates even, and this is used to justify local anger against the newcomers.

Over the course of our 150 interviews and our observation of dozens of party events, we have found it generally very rare to hear hatred, dislike, animosity or hostility towards migrants, and the situation was no different in the course of AfD electoral events or conversations with AfD-affiliated persons. Yet clear distinctions continue to be made between those who belong and those who do not, between those who have a right to be here and those who do not, but these distinctions are made with care, soberly. Hatred, as Nitzan Shoshan and Kathleen M. Blee have argued in regard to far-right politics, operates as a pejorative classification that has effects on those who are classified as 'hateful'.[43] In our research, hate was rarely explicitly expressed. We can explain this by reference to 'feeling rules'.

All political realms, as Arlie Hochschild has shown, are governed by feeling rules, imposing how one *should* feel (or at least, what one expresses about one's feelings) concerning particular political and social issues.[44] Expressions of hatred are, in many contexts, socially sanctioned. This include the German far-right political parties whose meetings we have observed. They do not express hatred of Muslims, dislike of Africans, distaste for gays and lesbians. Rather, they present themselves as first and foremost *besorgte Bürger* (concerned citizens).[45] If Hochschild is right, feelings are never just personal or subjective. In a political context, they are heavily sanctioned, policed by peers and regulated by social norms. Performing politics without expressing hatred is crucial for the AfD to transfer its messages to mixed audiences, and thus for creating a social space in which relations, identifications and attachments across the social spectrum can emerge and flourish.[46] And in this the AfD is far more effective than the more openly angry National Democrats were previously, not because their policy proposals differ markedly but because they are less forceful in their displays of feelings of malevolence for foreigners, migrants and feminists, scorn of liberals and revulsion against gays and lesbians.[47]

In the early autumn of 2019 three of the six federal states in Eastern Germany held regional parliamentary elections. For the state elections in Saxony, Thuringia and Brandenburg, polls showed the AfD competing for the majority of the vote in all three *Länder* and, throughout that year, the regional AfD organisations intensified their campaign efforts, in particular in rural areas. Some towns had no political posters except for AfD and the even more far-right party NPD. In an attempt to provide social spaces in which potential supporters are given the opportunity to connect with the political projects of the AfD, the party organised a scores of intimate gatherings and meetings with the interested public in clubhouses and community halls in hamlets, villages and towns all across Eastern Germany, focusing in particular on the rural areas. Not a week went by without an AfD event, and we were able to attend many of these gatherings in which we could observe the feeling rules dominating the party.[48]

In March 2019 Jörg Urban, the chairman of the AfD parliamentary group of Saxony, organised a meeting titled *Heimat Saxony* in Grosspösna, a borough of about five thousand inhabitants near Leipzig. About twenty people, mostly older men, attended. First, Urban presented the AfD manifesto. The subsequent discussion with the audience was a lament about the current state of politics, particularly the shortcomings of the current CDU-led government in Saxony.[49] Although the AfD had been elected to the Saxon parliament in the last election of 2014, this has so far not had much of an effect, members of the audience were complaining. Eventually, a member of the crowd addresses Jörg Urban directly: 'Maybe we need to be more courageous, maybe we need to start to talk to our fellow men about the AfD. It's not uncommon to withhold your opinions. But that's dangerous. This has been going on for decades, and now we're being dragged into the mud because we're saying it like it is.' Jörg Urban, standing in the middle of the room, addressed the man who was concerned about expressing his opinions: 'Just mention the principle of freedom of speech. What are you allowed to say today and what is forbidden? We need to establish a sensibility in order for people to start thinking: "Isn't it strange that I'm not allowed to say certain things? [...] How can it be that I can't talk normally without having to be afraid to be sanctioned in one way or another?"' An older man in the audience reacted: 'I was born in the GDR, and back then, you weren't allowed to say anything. Today, when you speak up, people say you're right-wing. [...] Today, we're facing the same circumstances as we did in the GDR. And people need to realise this! We're not right-wing, we're representing a politics that is in the true interest of the people!' This statement proved controversial, and Urban intervened: 'Yes, everything is getting worse. At the railway station at night, women aren't able to disembark the train on their own any more. Reality proves we need to engage with politics! And we need to have the courage to address problems and meet the people!' Jörg Dornau, another convenor of the meeting and AfD member, addressed the audience: 'This is why you need to talk to your children, talk to your grandchildren, your relatives, colleagues, neighbours. Awaken the people! Send them to the ballot boxes!'

What the participants were discussing – besides arguing that present-day Germany was in fact, in their view, a dictatorship – was how they are experiencing the dominant feeling rules.[50] Within the 'safe space' of an AfD party meeting, they felt able to talk freely about what concerned them, without having to fear 'any modes of social sanctioning' they claimed to be experiencing outside of this space.[51] Moreover, this space provided an affective affordance that 'resonated with the participants' and created a 'sense of connection' between a small group of 'like-minded people who share knowledge of *what is really going on*'.[52] These events allow for the performance of cultural intimacy, which, according to the anthropologist Michael Herzfeld, 'is a vital aspect of what constitutes [the] appeal' of populist politics.[53] What was at issue during the meeting then was not policies, but rather what it means to violate the common feeling rules valid by social covenant. The prohibition of expressing a sceptical view of migration politics was experienced by the attendant crowd as a debasement they insinuated was as unpleasant as the reprisals against dissidents in the GDR, which of course involved imprisonment and sometimes the death penalty. They are not interrupting each other for hyperbole. For racist language does come at a cost, keenly felt by these men in Grossbösna and elsewhere: the cost of losing out in the competition for economic resources, for respect and for their values to be heard. As Hochschild has shown, the now prevalent economic practices emphasise flexibility, self-promotion, mobility and diversity, and do not honour local involvement, family-orientation, resource-fulness and authenticity.[54]

The AfD appeals to heterogenous groups who have in common that they feel declassified in a myriad of ways: dis-empowered local elites, disappointed family men, Eastern Germans with devalued biographies and generally devalued workers and occupational groups. On top of these devalu-ations of values and of biographies, of these personal set-backs and disappointments, comes the devaluation through disapproval: whilst they are 'just saying it like it is', this is portrayed, in their minds by malevolent liberals and the biased media, as racism, backwardness and symptomatic of the Eastern German right. What is going on here, then, is an attempt to validate people's ways of expressing themselves by labelling those who would defame them as the real oppressors: it is not the AfD members who are racist, rather, those who label them so are oppressing the honest local population. In their eyes, 'these' people are merely 'traitors of the people' (*Volksverräter*). They resent having to feel shame at being associated with a party that is so vilified in public. As a young man on a train between Cottbus and Rietschen loudly proclaimed to a curious fellow passenger: 'They are called racist, but that cannot be true. I have been to AfD meetings. They are decent people.' The opposition between 'racist' or 'right-wing' and 'decent' is frequently made in an attempt to rewrite the feeling rules. For the 'decent' folk are 'misunderstood'. In their view, they are just trying to help the women who are now fearful of the dangers lurking in the dark. They stand on the side of the smallhold- ers who are fearful for their sheep. And to name the source of the danger, whether that is the male migrant or the wolf, is, they argue, not racist.

In telling and retelling these stories of fearful women and worried smallholders, AfD supporters are honing narra- tives that do not make them the bad guys. To put it another way:

> [All] political activity is determined by the stories we tell ourselves, the threats that we believe are most imminent and the voices around us to which we can relate the most. Far-right populist parties such as the AfD are actively work- ing to provide political narratives and identities as well as create spaces and opportunities for people to affirm and cer- tify their beliefs. Such work embraces the power of affective practices that contribute to legitimising the expression of far-right views in public realms, which had formerly been unacceptable.[55]

This goes for printed statements as well as public meet- ings. A recent study has shown that AfD statements to the press about crime focused virtually exclusively on crimes committed by those they portrayed as migrants (95 per cent) to an extent that did not match the realities of official crime statistics at all, thus exaggerating particular criminal phenomena while concealing others.[56] The authors of this study also pointed out that public perceptions of crime do not necessarily match the realities of official crime statistics and developments, but are, to a large extent, influenced by political debates and media reports. The AfD is clearly actively working on public perceptions of crime and immigrants, thereby transforming the feeling rules in regard to these political issues while simultaneously undermining people's trust in institutions and the press.

In its political communication, in media reports and on social media platforms, the AfD depicts sentiments of outrage at every single alleged act of crime committed by a visible minority or a migrant, although the most murderous person in the last twenty years has been a German serial killer, the former nurse Niels Högel, convicted of having killed eighty-five people – who is, of course, of no interest to far-right politics. Rather, the AfD obsesses over migrant crime. An infamous online map allows citizens to report crimes allegedly committed by a migrant or a visible minority.[57] Whilst certain crimes are highlighted in order to arouse indignation, other possibly outrageous incidents are ignored: When the CDU politician Walter Lübcke was shot on 2 June 2019 by a Western German far-right terrorist in Kassel, the AfD and other far-right groups framed the murder not as an outrageous act against civil society but as the logical consequence of a failing politics: 'He had it coming,' a PEGIDA protestor infamously stated on the national news.[58] We are witnessing a shift in a socially regulated distribution system of empathy. In order to feel no empathy, lives need to become valueless. One way of doing that is persistently talking about the 'criminal immigrant', 'the betrayer of the nation', 'being swamped by foreigners' and the 'surge of refugees'.

The increasing normalisation of far-right attitudes goes hand in hand with an increasing lack of shame for transgressing the boundaries of decency, argues the Austrian linguist Ruth Wodak. She sees us as being in the midst of a post-shame era rather than the 'post-truth era' frequently diagnosed.[59] *Post-shame* implies a transformation of affective constellations and registers of feeling.[60] Thus, the AfD does not use emotions to manipulate or 'seduce' people to adapt far-right views; it opens up 'enabling spaces in which people can freely express their far-right views without the need to "feel bad" about them or fear social sanctions'.[61]

The affective politics of the far right and their underlying narratives contribute to the promotion and normalisation of racist discourse and practices. The rural regions in Eastern Germany are especially affected by this persistent normalisation, as there is little 'polite society' to insist on maintaining decorum. Slowly, but persistently, far-right attitudes have become more socially acceptable and more capable of mobilisation.

Only those who listen hear the howl of the wolf

In Oberwiesenthal town, where Saxony borders on the Czech Republic, the Saxon Ministry for the Environment, Agriculture and Geology organised an information meeting open to the interested public on a warm summer evening in June 2019.[62] Representatives of the Ministry, Vanessa Ludwig, Matthias Rau and Ulrich Klausnitzer, tried to inform the audience on the topic of the returning wolves. Some attending clearly expressed the view that they did not want or need to be educated on the topic. Whilst Vanessa Ludwig explained that, currently, eighteen wolf packs live in Saxony, and seventy-five are counted Germany-wide, some people in the audience shook their heads, others crossed their arms in front of their upper bodies. A man said to her: 'Your statistics are wrong! Killed grazing animals are not included. And a second mistake: You're talking about wolves. That is wrong! The genes of wolves and wolf dogs are only 2.5 per cent apart. The wolves are being bred and let free, and you don't record hybrids at all!' The speaker Ludwig tried to navigate the questions from the audience as best as she could, but without any success in convincing them of 'the facts'.

When Matthias Rau subsequently tried to give his talk concerning the protection measures available to farmers for their livestock, he did not get far. Minutes into his presentation, a local farmer and his wife interrupted him: 'I'd like to share a story about how well your wolf office is working, if nobody here is against it. Well? Okay then.' Rau, who already knew the farmer, because he had worked on evaluating a case of his killed sheep recently, tried to shut him down: 'Your case was very special, we can talk about it later.' Which was enough for the farmer to raise his voice and shout: 'You want to stop me from telling it like it is? Then leave, Mister Rau, if you can't bear to hear it. It's your responsibility, and the people have the right to find out what happens if they're attacked by a wolf, and who is ultimately responsible!' Rau said: 'There's no need to wash one's dirty laundry in public. Your case was in May and the killing was your first killing.' The farmer and his wife shouted back in unison: 'You're not letting us speak!'

And the wife explained: 'When we had our animals killed, I dialled your number and the assessor said to me, "I just need to finish my meal." *Four* hours later, he came! And all he said was, "Your fence is not in order."' And her husband added: 'You can spread your lies all you want, but if we are telling the truth … We're not in the GDR, we live in a democracy. You can tell the media anything you want, but the people here need to hear the truth!' At the end of a long discussion between several members of the audience, including laments about taxpayers' money going to waste and demands for shooting all wolves, a woman addressed the Ministry representatives with: 'You're sitting on your balconies in your fancy cities, and no one of you ever saw what such a killing actually looks like, with the eyes ripped out, the heads flayed, and the sheep breathing through their windpipes because they can't die.'

Information events on the wolf issue almost always end up like this. The audiences in these rural regions, made up of farmers, hunters and local residents, develop affective dynamics during these events and, in the end, the information provided by official authorities does not matter, the people are left feeling enraged and, significantly, reassured in their rage. In particular, they feel reassured that, in principle, it seems, the government is lying to them, and that wolves are part of an elaborate scheme to harm the rural regions, as they are deliberately 'being bred and let free' in their homeland. In asides during such meetings, during wolf tours and in pub talks with strangers, in particular in Saxony, the view was widespread that wolves had been introduced by malevolent urban dwellers by the truck-load, flown in by helicopters into military exclusion zones, or in the boots of unmarked cars.[63] People expecting a conspiracy cannot be reasoned with using factual information.

More successful, by far, are the far-right parties such as the AfD and its splinters when they are strategically tending to the topics that the rural population is enraged about. In their campaign events in the rural regions in the East we have attended, the AfD politicians show that they are present in rural hamlets and boroughs – unlike any other party – and that they are listening to citizens' concerns without judgement, understanding the reasons for their rage. Simultaneously, they provide narratives that make sense of these resentments and channel them towards those 'responsible' for all their misery. It's never the economy, globalisation or bad politics, it's always the 'elite', the government, the Greens and those in the cities. The AfD takes up the resentments, amplifies them and provides an affective-narrative solution, confirming the people's suspicions that 'the government', chancellor Merkel or the liberals and Greens could be 'behind all this' – a strategy that proved to be dangerously effective in the campaigns during the election year 2019.

As the AfD federal MP Karsten Hilse stated in his Bundestag speech on the wolf that we quoted in the Introduction: the government has left 'the people alone with their worries'. Now AfD politicians all across the East are rushing to listen to and care about these worries, and trying to offer a solution, and in this process journalists, scholars and politicians from other parties are increasingly suggesting the liberal political forces should do the same. All in all, *we should listen to the people in the East and understand their misery* is essentially the claim in the books published by the Social Democrats Petra Köpping and Frank Richter, which we summarised in Chapter 1. But could listening really be the solution to undermine the AfD's electoral successes? On the contrary, argued author İmran Ayata:

A common misconception is that you need only to listen closely to and understand the Bautzeners, Dresdeners and Heidenauers and all other citizens who are experiencing social decline or fear for their future. For years, we have been taking the worries and fears of 'the people' seriously. More specifically, media and politicians constantly claim that we must take the middle class's fear of social decline seriously, even if they articulate it in a racist way. The fact that refugees are associated with long-standing social problems – that's exactly what this instrumentalisation of listening is all about.[64]

The key word here is 'future'. The future in many Eastern German regions *is* precarious and uncertain. Too many people have moved away, whilst those who stay are voting for the AfD. Now the AfD provides a vision of the future that resonates with the people who are staying. They say, your future is endangered by the wolves, and by the migrants. They politicise the future and make use of the affective mechanisms of anxiety and hope.

6

Sheep in wolves' clothing?

> The National Socialist Specter, in this account, exposes its sinister face in the crevices of a disintegrating social fabric, and it is here that the battle against it would have to be waged.
>
> Nitzan Shoshan, *The Management of Hate*[1]

Eastern Germany is haunted by the spectre of the Nazi, so goes the dominant account, because it is caught in developments of globalisation and depopulation, deindustrialisation and the masculinisation of rural culture. The federal and local governments attempt to tame the new nationalism by pouring ever more resources into (re-)building this social fabric. Resources are allocated to youth workers located in youth clubs, schools, gaming rooms, self-managed cafés; to schools for teachers so that they can engage in adult education in order to recognise young people straying to the far right and bring them 'back' to better, more democratic, more civic values.

Teenagers are assessed and policed in terms of the music they hear, the clothes they wear, their school performance, extra-curricular activities, tattoos and of course the statements they make in a public (school) context. Resources are also allocated to non-profit organisations that they may conduct research on the rise of right-wing youth cultures, that they may reach out to young people in rural areas, formulate intervention strategies and provide expert consulting services to others.[2] And yet, the rise of the right – in terms of voting behaviour, in terms of the rise of vigilante groups, far-right terrorist cells, arson attacks against refugee homes, anti-migrant demonstrations – is relentless.

However, the rise of the right is not led by political parties or organised initiatives. We have shown that the AfD does not use emotions to manipulate or seduce people to adapt far-right views. Rather, the AfD and other fringe right-wing parties are galvanising politically unhappy members of the population by three strategies: they enable the expression of unseeming emotions like anger, hate and disgust; they reduce complexity by using figures that justify these emotions, like migrants and wolves; and they make use of the sort of identity politics that gives recognition without merit.

First, they open up enabling spaces in which people can express their far-right views without having to feel bad about them, and without having to fear social sanctions. A culture of resentment and of impunity makes people find occasions to express their displeasure with the present and their fear for the future. Such occasions include spaces organised by new and right-wing political parties, where they can articulate their anger. This articulation of anger, resentment and loss needs an object, but the object of fear can be chosen fairly arbitrarily – the discourses meander from the wolf to the migrant and back again. Both justify articulations of anger against those 'Greens' who allegedly imported them. And, second, the AfD in a genial reduction of complexity takes up these emotions by stoking further fears of a decline of order, civilisation, peace and general cultural demise.

And they do this in particular by using signal events for their cause.

Signal incidents involving homicide and sexual violence by stigmatised minorities are successful mobilisers for public displays of animosity to migration and the government. Such events provide a bridge between personal fears of violence and projections of a threatening alien force, linking one's personal anxiety with the political interpretation that German society, imagined as overwhelmingly peaceful, is infiltrated by potent and brutal intruders against whom the liberals are unwilling to protect us.

The wolf and the migrant are thus figures that signify sorrow and fear at the (perceived) loss of sovereignty and at the betrayal they feel from the elites: the 'Greens' 'inviting' strangers into this land are doing so in keeping with EU rules. They stand for the globalisation or Europeanisation of policies, and this felt loss of sovereignty is causing feelings of doom – and sentiments of impending doom have long served to galvanise resistance fighters. And resistance against the GDR long took the form of neo-Nazi organising, the worst provocation against the self-avowedly socialist state that spoke of itself as having overcome all forms of capitalist and nationalist thinking.[3] So this form of resistance has some continuities with the GDR, though it is reductionist to deduce that it was the GDR that caused the sort of authoritarian and racist thinking prevalent on the far right. Rather, being a neo-Nazi has anti-establishmentarian connotations in rural areas.

So why is anti-establishmentarianism prevalent in rural areas? And why is it more prevalent in Eastern Germany? First, we noted a cultural, political and social devaluation of everything Eastern. The people are considered premodern, whiny and authoritarian, the indigenous products exotic, the workforce undervalued and badly paid. Second, salaried employees have very few chances of moving up the career ladder, where most positions remain steadfastly in Western hands. And third, there is no political party representing the interests of those who are not socially and geographically mobile. So we have here the three crises Andreas Reckwitz has called the crises of our age: the crisis of recognition, the crisis of self-improvement and the crisis of politics.[4]

All these crises are met with an identity politics that focuses not on the fickle topics of individuation, self-improvement and flexibility, which are values less prevalent in rural areas. Rather, the new identity politics are conservative and nationalist: valuing traditional families rather than flexibility, valuing the nation over self-improvement, valuing reliability over transnational networking. Both traditionalism and nationalism have the advantages of conferring recognition on their proponents without achievement. This makes both sources for recognition risible to some, and yet the only sources of recognition available to others. And this in turn provokes a recurring cycle of devaluation and self-revaluation of a class sometimes called 'left-behind', a cycle that is not simple to dissolve or suspend.

This brings us to the third strategy of the AfD and similar movements and parties: Eastern German identity has developed into a political battleground, and far-right politicians have discovered that such an identity can be reinvented. In this context the Eastern German identity is not left behind, but the vanguard of a new, better, more traditional and less transnational Germany. A Germany of the good old 'German values', valuing constancy, traditional family values, a solidarity among cultural equals. Though of course, 'cultural equals' become ethnicised and racialised:

the old logics of 'being German' as a matter of descent. And this is a satisfying solution, many seem to feel, for the devaluation of values and lives experienced at the hands of the Western Germans and their media. The people thus collectively aggrieved are tempted to label those who would defame them as the real oppressors: in this reversal of disapproval, it is not the far right or the AfD voters who are racist, rather those who label them so are oppressing the honest local population.

Ultimately, despite those who would want to overthrow the government, eliminate all migrants and wolves, and 'take our country back again', much of the fight is one with a fundamentally democratic tone. The rallying cry 'This is a democracy, we are the people, and this is what we want!' that we heard with variations from the very first wolf-related meeting in Lusatia is a democratic impetus. As Philip Manow has argued recently with reference to Hegel and Kant, it is one of the paradoxes of democracy that the rabble is always already excluded, in at least two ways: first, the legitimation processes in a democracy are based on the legitimate claim to rule, which has been acquired by some more than others, namely by those who work, as opposed to those who profit from the work of others or from charity or welfare. And secondly, the logics of representation favour those who are, in a figurative sense, *representable*; the others do not vote, and their interests are not deemed worthy of representation.[5] What we are seeing now, with the rise of the new populist parties, is thus a democratisation of politics, to the detriment of the democracy as we know it now. The new nationalist parties are not doing a better job at representing interests, but they are good at representing those whose affects are too uncivilised, whose views of the 'elites' too harsh, whose lust for a new order

too impetuous and whose enthusiasm for exclusion too bar-
baric. Thus, they want to be like the wolves in parliament,
as Goebbels had described the National Socialists, but they
remain largely irrelevant, belittled and ineffective, sheep,
that is, in wolves' clothing.

So for a number of reasons, this democratic impetus
remains loud and yet unheard given a political climate in
which they feel utterly disregarded and disdained – precisely
in part, of course, of deviating from the officially prescribed
discourse on the German nation. So their solution to their
lack of recognition is a poisoned chalice: the nation provides
them with recognition that is unearned, as all nationalism
does, and solves in part the problem that they feel their
region, their values and their identities are treated with
contempt. But this solution in the German context violates
a basic consensus that had been established after 1968 about
what it means, and what it doesn't mean, to be German:
you cannot and must not articulate pride in the German
nation *as such*, as this is interpreted as disregarding the
National Socialist genocides and expansionisms, in particular towards Poland. But this post-1968 ethics is a distinctly
West German way of handling the past. As Stephan Locke
pointed out, flying the German flag during the GDR period
meant being in favour of a united nation, not stupidly celebrating a horrific past. Nationalisms in the Western and
Eastern Germanys have different connotations, and so the
(Western) contempt for Eastern pride is felt as if it were a
mangling of the innocent intentions of Eastern denizens. In
this respect there is only one valid interpretation: according
to the status quo, the East has the wrong one, tragically, we
must add: again.

But of course, the context is not ambivalent at all: since
the GDR period, and in particular in the 1990s, neo-Nazi

networks and youth cultures have thrived in many rural and suburban areas in the East (not only there, of course, but with a greater density).[6] The East is also home to important terrorist networks of people dreaming of a new revolution, a second uprising against a dictatorship.[7] Their problem is that the current government, many nationalists argue, merely pretends to be conservative, but it is, in fact, a new form of socialism, this time, profiting feminists, migrants and queers. And as such, they say, the current government is just another dictatorship,[8] and only Eastern Germans are savvy enough to recognise a 'liberal dictatorship' for what it is.

This explains two of the questions we started the book with: Why are some so susceptible to right-wing offers of a politics of fear, and why do they cluster in the East? That leaves us with the last two of the questions we started with – what functions do tropes of the wolf fulfil, and why do right-wing terrorist organisations, as well as leading national socialists and Nazi sympathizers, celebrate wolves? On a superficial level, we found that there is an appetite for blaming the liberal asylum and immigration policies that have made the 'import of the wolf' and the 'Muslim invasion' possible in the first place, as they are allegedly benefiting those undeserving and harming 'our own'; and this harm is leading to a calamity, as the *telos* is to replace the ethnic European. Those who are to blame for the great replacement of the German people include everyone who renders the replacement possible or does not oppose it, that is, politicians, the establishment, liberals, greens, leftists and the naive, duped and/or brainwashed people who have not yet been awakened – and are commonly referred to by white nationalists as 'sleeping sheep'. Both these 'inva-sions' must be resisted in order to secure the survival of the nation – that is, the nation imagined as an ethnic people, as a homogeneous cultural entity, or as a superior civilisation. The wolf stands for an impending catastrophe, but also for the resilience that must be mustered against it.

The *affective* functions of wolf tropes range from mobilising *fear* – one common discourse turns wolves into weapons against the local populations, and migrants and refugees into presumed Islamist fanatics and terrorists, into knife murderers and rapists – to *antagonising* well-established parties and the government. But an important affect is also showing *care* for the girls threatened by wolves or disgusted by mangled sheep, for all victims of the 'great transformation', including *our* traditional landscapes, *our* sense of security, the natural order and, in particular, those people and animals that have *always* lived here. The AfD and its splinter parties are particularly active in rural areas, enacting themselves there as parties that truly care, as opposed to the cosmopolitan urbanites focused on queer, feminist and animal rights who consider themselves our elites. Gestures of care lead to *solidarity* and a sense of representation. Such indications of inclusion come with reminders of exclusion: It's mainly about the wolves not belonging here. In negotiating the solidarity, they are answering another question, namely, who is part of the *demos* and who is not, who and which animals really belong in Saxony, Lusatia, or Germany and who is an unwelcome and potentially dangerous intruder. The wolf in many contexts stands not (merely) for a predatory animal but for an occasion for urban dwellers to patronise, belittle and pick on hunters and other good country folk. The urban centres and their cosmopolitan dwellers thus have one more occasion to develop their 'culture of condescension', and the cycle of devaluation continues.

For those people sympathising with the offers made by right-wing populist parties, democracy in fact *is* in crisis; not because of the rise of a phenomenon academic observers call right-wing populism but because the voters for these splinter parties feel politically unheard and ignored in their needs – in their community, in Germany and in Europe. Hence the phrase 'cruel optimism' as integral to the promise of representative democracy: the promise of power of the people – a promise that more often than not remains vague and empty.

We are therefore witnessing a return to nationalist political thinking by those who feel unheard in their hope to limit migration and the spread of predators: keep out (most of) the wolves, keep out the (Muslim) migrants, and preserve the local ways of life, for the deer, for 'our' women and children. But we also need to keep in mind that the wolf-affected regions, particularly in the East, are regions rife with structural problems. But as all political utterances coming from the East are discredited as right-wing, wrong-headed, ungrateful and ignorant, there is no way of articulating these demands successfully, so it seems. People complain about wolves, they are always heard when they talk about wolves. To summarise, first, the wolf is a protagonist in the politics of fear that helps far-right populist parties such as the AfD appear as a party that cares for the needs and worries of the rural population, while simultaneously tapping into widespread anti-immigration, anti-urban and anti-government resentments. Second, the wolf tends to be conflated with particular conceptions of *Heimat*, whereby elements of the far-right blood-and-soil ideology seem to thrive. Third, with the help of the wolf, different conceptions of invasive species and alien populations are being expressed, while the value of *Heimat* landscapes and territories are being elevated. And fourth, the wolf figure assembles an array of conceptions of an alleged invasive and domineering foe, among them Greens, urban dwellers and Western Germans.

The wolf, then, is part and parcel of a dualism between good and evil nature, between order and chaos, civilisation and barbarism. In refusing to side with civilised man, Hobbes's wolf man has free range to endanger us all. To resist the wolf or wolfman is to resist returning to the state of nature. So even though, in a literal sense, the wolf is no threat to anyone who is neither sheep nor deer, as an anthropomorphous object the wolf becomes accessible to political discourse.

The wolf is thus not a political cipher that harnesses fear and resentments as such, yet, when figuring in far-right discourses, it takes on a range of meanings that relate to doom, annihilation, death and destruction. It is thus not the wolf that is like the migrant but the migrant who takes on similar meanings to the cipher of the wolf. In far-right politics, the wolf thus serves as a figure to construe a (predominantly) rural population as vulnerable to infiltrating populations of predators who have been invited in by urban dwellers who remain luxuriously far removed from the consequences of their decisions.

Notes

NOTES TO INTRODUCTION: WOLF POLITICS

1 All translations from the German, unless otherwise stated, are by the authors.

2 The EU Habitats Directive (Council Directive 92/43/EEC on the Conservation of Natural Habitats and of Wild Fauna and Flora) was adopted in 1992 and assures the conservation of endangered animal and plant species in the territories of the EU member states. The wolf (*Canis lupus*) is listed among approximately one thousand species in the directive's Annexes.

3 Ravens kill lambs: see P. Carstens, 'Raben für mehr tote Schafe verantwortlich als Wölfe', *GEO* (19 November 2018), URL: www.geo.de/natur/tierwelt/19945-rtkl-tausende-tote-laemmer-raben-fuer-mehr-tote-schafe-verantwortlich-als [Accessed 17 May 2020]. A shepherds' lobby group makes the point forcefully that it is the wolf that is to blame for the decline in the business: see Förderverein der Deutschen Schafhaltung, 'Deutsche Schäfer sind fassungslos und wütend: "Warum lässt uns die Gesellschaft im Stich?"', *Wir Lieben Schafe: Pressemitteilungen* (29 April 2020), URL: www.wir-lieben-schafe.com/pressemitteilungen/ [Accessed 17 May 2020]. In a press release from September 2019, it points out that peripatetic shepherds are becoming extinct; and that 2018 saw a reduction of sheep-holding to 9,500 businesses with at least twenty sheep each, which is a reduction of 16 per cent over ten years. Fewer than a thousand full-time shepherds remain: see A. Deter, 'Schäfer in Not: Zahl der Berufsschäfer jetzt unter 1000!', *topagrar online* (6 March 2018), URL: www.topagrar.com/management-und-politik/news/schaefer-in-not-zahl-der-berufssc haefer-jetzt-unter-1000-9410439.html [Accessed 17 May 2020].

Notes

The general population seems to be quite interested in wolf conservation, however, as the Nature and Biodiversity Conservation Union (German: NABU), also a lobby group, claims to have established, see NABU, 'Forsa-Umfrage zum Wolf: Zustimmung in der Bevölkerung bleibt hoch. Miller: Klima für die Akzeptanz des Wolfes ist nach wie vor gut', *Nabu Presseportal* (6 March 2018), URL: www.presseportal.de/pm/6347/3928649 [Accessed 17 May 2020].

4 Pseudonym. Throughout this book, we mark with *those names which are pseudonyms, often people who are not political entrepreneurs, or marginal ones who might have incriminated themselves in the course of an interview. Our business is not to uncover hidden truths, expose people for unguarded but public statements or breach interviewees' trust in talking to us openly, but to explicate open truths that may go ignored because of the ignominy of the circles in which they take place.

5 Frohnmaier, M. (26.08.2018): 'Wenn der Staat die Bürger nicht mehr schützen kann, gehen die Menschen auf die Straße und schützen sich selber. Ganz einfach! Heute ist es Bürgerpflicht, die todbringende "Messermigration" zu stoppen! Es hätte deinen Vater, Sohn oder Bruder treffen können!' URL: https://twitter.com/Frohnmaier_AfD/status/1033806135990644744.

6 See www.express.de/news/skandal-forderung-afd-politiker-marcus-pretzell-will-fluechtlinge-mit-waffen-stoppen--23094688.

7 See https://netzpolitik.org/2019/wir-veroeffentlichen-das-verfass ungsschutz-gutachten-zur-afd/.

8 Quoted in A. Lang, *The Blue Fairy Book* (London: Longmans, Green and Co., 1889), 53.

9 K. Hilse, 'Wolfsmanagement und -monitoring', *Deutscher Bundestag: Parlamentsfernsehen* [Video file] (21 February 2019), URL: www.bundestag.de/mediathek?videoid=7328919#url=L2rl ZGlhdGhla292ZXJsYXk/dmlkZW9pZD03MzI4OTE5JnppZGGVv aWQ9NzMyODkxOSZ2aWRlb2lkPTczMjg5MTk=&mod=mediat hek [Accessed 24 November 2019].

10 J. Retterath, 'Volk', in I. Haar, M. Fahlbusch and M. Berg (eds), *Handbuch der völkischen Wissenschaften* (München: Personen – Institutionen – Forschungsprogramme – Stiftungen, 2008), 1185.

11 Barthes (2013), quoted in C. Kølvraa, 'Wolves in sheep's clothing? The Danish far right and "wild nature"', in B. Forchtner (ed.), *The far right and the environment. Politics, discourse and communication* (London and New York: Routledge, 2020), 109.

12 R. Wodak, *The politics of fear* (London: Sage, 2015), 1.

Notes

13 However, since 1950 there have been nine lethal wolf attacks in other regions of Europe. In four cases rabies was involved.

14 Cf. D. Kummetz, J. Schaar, N. Hotsch and J. Jacobsen, 'Interaktive Karte: Wölfe in Schleswig-Holstein', *NDR 1 Welle Nord* (27 February 2020), URL: www.ndr.de/nachrichten/schleswig-hol stein/Interaktive-Karte-Woelfe-in-Schleswig-Holstein,wolf3736. html [Accessed 17 May 2020].

15 In this regard we have been considerably inspired by Arlie R. Hochschild's study *Strangers in Their Own Land* (New York; London: The New Press, 2016) and her ethnographic method of unraveling the 'deep story' behind the rise of the right in the United States of America.

16 P. Manow: 'Demokratisierung der Demokratie', *Merkur* (22 November 2019), URL: www.merkur-zeitschrift.de/2019/11/22/ demokratisierung-der-demokratie/ [Accessed 18 February 2020].

17 A. Appadurai, 'Democracy fatigue', in H. Geiselberger (ed.), *The great regression* (Cambridge; Malden: Polity Press, 2017), 1.

18 S. Levitsky and D. Ziblatt, *How democracies die* (New York: Broadway Books, 2018).

19 Y. Mounk, *The people vs. democracy* (Cambridge, MA: Harvard University Press, 2018).

20 C. Mouffe, *For a left populism* (London; New York: Verso, 2018).

21 A. R. Hochschild, *Strangers in their own land* (New York; London: The New Press, 2016).

22 J. Gest, *The New Minority* (New York: Oxford University Press, 2016), 170.

23 We summarised these hypotheses in M. Dellenbaugh-Losse, J. Homeyer, J. Leser and R. Pates, 'Toxische Orte? Faktoren der regionalen Anfälligkeit für völkischen Nationalismus', in L. Berg and J. Üblacker (eds), *Rechtes Denken – Rechte Räume* (Bielefeld: transcript, 2020), 47–82.

24 L. Berlant, *Cruel optimism* (Durham, NC: Duke University Press, 2011).

25 Wodak, *The politics of fear.*

26 K. Hilse, 'Bundesnaturschutzgesetz und Wolfsmanagement', *Deutscher Bundestag: Parlamentsfernsehen* [Video file] (24 October 2019), URL: www.bundestag.de/mediathek?videoid=7397 423#url=L21lZGlhdGhla292ZXJsYXk/dmlkZW9pZDo3Mzk3NDI zJnZpZGVvaWQ9NzM5NzQyMw==&mod=mediathek [Accessed 10 May 2020].

27 M. Feola, 'Fear and loathing in democratic times', *Political Studies* 64 (2015), 53.

Notes

28 P. Virilio, *The administration of fear* (Los Angeles: Semiotext(e), 2012).

29 P. Köpping, *Integriert doch erst mal uns!* (Berlin: Ch. Links Verlag, 2018).

Notes to Chapter 1: The 'East': Depopulation, deindustrialisation, colonialism

1 We interviewed Frank Richter in Leipzig in November 2018 for a BBC Radio 4 documentary.

2 The research is summarised in W. J. Patzelt, 'Mängel in der Responsivität oder Störungen in der Kommunikation? Deutschlands Repräsentationslücke und die AfD', *ZParl Zeitschrift für Parlamentsfragen* 49:4 (2018), 885–895.

3 F. Rösel, 'Die Wucht der deutschen Teilung wird völlig unterschätzt', *Ifo Dresden berichtet* 3 (2019), 23–25.

4 H. Berking, 'Experiencing reunification. An East German village after the fall of the Wall', in L. Rudolph and J. K. Jacobsen (eds) *Experiencing the state* (Oxford: Oxford University Press, 2006), 143–164.

5 Ibid., 149.

6 W. Engler, *Die ungewollte Moderne. Ost-West-Passagen* (Frankfurt am Main: edition Suhrkamp, 1995).

7 Berking, 'Experiencing reunification', 148.

8 W. Engler, *Die zivilisatorische Lücke* (Frankfurt am Main: edition Suhrkamp, 1992).

9 Berking, 'Experiencing reunification', 148.

10 Ibid., 146.

11 Numerous reports discuss this, e.g. E. Lohse, 'Westdeutsche AfD Politiker. Geliebter Anführer aus dem Lager des Feindes', *FAZ* (3 August 2019), URL: www.faz.net/aktuell/politik/inland/wieso-es-afd-wortfuehrern-nuetzt-wenn-sie-westdeutsche-sind-16315709.html [Accessed 3 November 2019]; Merkur, *Ost-AfD im Steigflug – und viele Westdeutsche am Schalthebel* (14 June 2019), URL: www.merkur.de/politik/ost-afd-im-steigflug-und-viele-westdeutsche-am-schalthebel-zr-12441394.html [Accessed 25 October 2019].

12 P. Köpping, *Integriert doch erstmal uns! Eine Streitschrift für den Osten* (Berlin: Ch. Links Verlag, 2018), 118–119; H. Best, 'Die Ausgangslage 1989/90: Elitenwechsel oder Elitenreproduktion?', in Deutsche Gesellschaft e.V. (ed.), *Ostdeutsche Eliten. Träume, Wirklichkeiten und Perspektiven* (Online Publikation: Deutsche Gesellschaften e.V., 2017), 36–45, 36; R. Kollmorgen, 'Ostdeutsche

in den Eliten. Problemdimensionen und Zukunftsperspektiven', in Deutsche Gesellschaft e.V. (ed.), *Ostdeutsche Eliten. Träume, Wirklichkeiten und Perspektiven* (Online Publikation: Deutsche Gesellschaften e.V., 2017), 54–65, 61.

13 Quoted from Bundestag, *Bundestag Document 11/8472* (Berlin: Bundestag, 1991).

14 Quoted in N. Pötzl, *Der Treuhand-Komplex. Legenden. Fakten. Emotionen* (Hamburg: kursbuch.edition, 2019), 74.

15 E. Most, *Fünfzig Jahre im Auftrag des Kapitals* (Berlin: Das Neue Berlin, 2009), 163.

16 G. Winkler, *Sozialreport 1994. Daten und Fakten zur sozialen Lage in den neuen Bundesländern* (Berlin: GSFP, 1994), 88.

17 I.-S. Kowalczuk, *Die Übernahme. Wie Ostdeutschland Teil der Bundesrepublik wurde* (München: C.H. Beck, 2019), 56.

18 Ibid., 61.

19 Ibid., 274.

20 Bpb – Bundeszentrale für politische Bildung (Federal Agency for Civic Education), 'Das Vermögen der DDR und die Privatisierung durch die Treuhand' (2015), URL: www.bpb.de/geschichte/deutsche-ein heit/zahlen-und-fakten-zur-deutschen-einheit/211280/das-verm oegen-der-ddr-und-die-privatisierung-durch-die-treuhand [Accessed 17 May 2020].

21 The East Germans arguably gained an environmental clean-up, solidarity in gaining immediate access to an advanced welfare and medical insurance scheme they had not paid into, pension plans and a new infrastructure. The West Germans paid as a collective, but as individuals many had new career options, investment opportunities in real estate and land, and perhaps a sense of victory. But in the current political climate it's not the gains that are in focus.

22 Pötzl, *Der Treuhand-Komplex*, 61.

23 The authors are currently working on the research project *Strangers in their own land* funded by the German Federal Ministry for Education and Research (BMBF) in which we explore the ramifications of this sense of loss on the willingness to integrate migrants.

24 M. Hartshorn Dellenbaugh, *Landscape changes in East Berlin after 1989. A comprehensive grounded theory analysis through three case studies.* Dissertation (Berlin: Humboldt-Universität zu Berlin, 2013), 11.

25 See M. Decker, 'Bpb-Chef über westdeutsche Dominanz: Es fehlen Übersetzer', *Berliner Zeitung* (31 October 2017), URL: www. berliner-zeitung.de/politik/bpb-chef-ueber-westdeutsche-dominanz-

Notes

es-fehlen-uebersetzer-kultureller-differenzen--28746484 [Accessed 25 October 2019].

26 Ibid.

27 F. den Hertog, *Minderheit im eigenen Land? zur gesellschaftlichen Position der Ostdeutschen in der gesamtdeutschen Realität* (Frankfurt am Main; New York: Campus, 2004). See also W. Dümcke and F. Vilmar, *Kolonialisierung der DDR. Kritische Anmerkungen und Alternativen des Einigungsprozesses* (Münster: Agend, 1995); S. Bollinger, U. Busch, D. Dahn and F. Vilmar (eds), *Zehn Jahre Vereinigungspolitik: Kritische Bilanz und humane Alternativen* (Berlin: Dr. W. Weist, 2000); P. Cooke, *Representing East Germany since unification. From colonization to nostalgia* (Oxford: Berg, 2005).

28 For example, M. Böick, *Die Treuhand. Idee – Praxis – Erfahrung 1990–1994* (Göttingen: Wallstein-Verlag, 2018).

29 For example, R. Kollmorgen, 'Außenseiter der Macht. Ostdeutsche in den bundesdeutschen Eliten', in U. Busch and M. Thomas (eds), *Ein Vierteljahrhundert Deutsche Einheit. Facetten einer unvollendeten Integration* (Berlin: trafo Wissenschaftsverlag, 2015), 189–220.

30 For example: W. Engler and J. Hensel, *Wer wir sind: die Erfahrung, ostdeutsch zu sein* (Berlin, Aufbau, 2018); A. Lettrari, C. Nestler and N. Troi-Boeck (eds), *Die Generation der Wendekinder: Elaboration eines Forschungsfeldes* (Wiesbaden: Springer, 2016). See also R. Pates and M. Schochow (eds), *Der 'Ossi': Mikropolitische Studien über einen symbolischen Ausländer* (Wiesbaden: Springer VS, 2013).

31 D. Kubiak, 'Der Fall "Ostdeutschland". "Einheitsfiktion" als Herausforderung für die Integration am Fallbeispiel der Ost-West-Differenz', *Zeitschrift für Vergleichende Politikwissenschaft* 12 (2018), 25–42; N. Foroutan, F. Kalter, C. Canan and M. Simon, *Ost-Migrantische Analogien I. Konkurrenz um Anerkennung* (Berlin: DeZIM-Institut, 2019), 4.

32 See: R. Pates, 'Einleitung – Der "Ossi" als symbolischer Ausländer', in R. Pates and M. Schochow (eds), *Der 'Ossi'. Mikropolitische Studien über einen symbolischen Ausländer* (Wiesbaden: Springer VS, 2013), 7–20; T. Ahbe, 'Die Konstruktion der Ostdeutschen. Diskursive Spannungen, Stereotype und Identitäten seit 1989', *Aus Politik und Zeitgeschichte* B41–42/2004 (2004), 12–22.

33 A brief overview of the genealogies and actors (and their location) of research on East Germany can be found in L. Probst, '"Wendekinder" schlagen ein neues Kapitel der DDR- und

Ostdeutschlandforschung auf', in A. Lettrari, C. Nestler and N. Troi-Boeck (eds), *Die Generation der Wendekinder. Elaboration eines Forschungsfeldes* (Wiesbaden: Springer, 2016), 31–36.

34 Köpping, *Integriert doch erst mal uns*, 52.
35 Ibid., 19–25.
36 Ibid., 25.
37 F. Richter, *Hört endlich zu! Weil Demokratie Auseinandersetzung braucht* (Berlin: Ullstein, 2018), 30.
38 Ibid., 34–35.
39 This is the title of Kowalczuk's essay on the *Treuhand*: *The Takeover. How Eastern Germany Joined the Federal Republic* published in 2019.
40 Quoted in Pötzl, *Der Treuhand-Komplex*, 9.
41 Ibid., 48.
42 Ibid., 54.
43 Ibid., 70.
44 Ibid., 11.
45 C. Babka von Gostomski, B. Küpper and W. Heitmeyer, 'Fremdenfeindlichkeit in den Bundesländern. Die schwierige Lage in Ostdeutschland', in W. Heitmeyer (ed.), *Edition Suhrkamp: Vol. 2484. Deutsche Zustände, Folge 5* (Frankfurt am Main: Suhrkamp, 2007), 102–128.
46 IWH, *Vereintes Land – drei Jahrzehnte nach dem Mauerfall* (Halle: Leibniz-Institut für Wirtschaftsforschung, 2019).
47 See K. J. Cramer, *The politics of resentment: Rural consciousness in Wisconsin and the rise of Scott Walker* (Chicago; London: University of Chicago Press, 2016); Hochschild, *Strangers in their own land*.
48 S. Mau, *Lütten Klein. Leben in der ostdeutschen Transformationsgesellschaft* (Berlin: Suhrkamp, 2019), 194.
49 Ibid., 195.
50 Ibid., 197.
51 M. S. Kimmel, *Angry white men: American masculinity at the end of an era* (New York: Nation Books, 2017).
52 D. Zuckerberg, *Not all dead white men. Classics and misogyny in the digital age* (Cambridge, MA: Harvard University Press, 2018), 12–13.
53 See www.ft.com/content/05baa6ae-86dd-11e9-a028-86cea8523dc2.
54 Ibid.
55 Interview with Petra Köpping, Minister for Integration in Saxony, in Dresden in November 2018.
56 Interview with Stefan Locke, correspondent for the *Frankfurter Allgemeine Zeitung*, in Dresden in November 2018, on the

Notes

occasion of the BBC programme. The interview was conducted in English.

57 K. Brauer, 'Bowling mit Wölfen. Rurale Gemeinden zwischen demographischem Untergang und (sozial-)kapitaler Zukunft', in U. Fachinger and H. Künemund (eds), *Gerontologie und ländlicher Raum. Lebensbedingungen, Veränderungsprozesse und Gestaltungsmöglichkeiten* (Wiesbaden: Springer VS, 2015), 48.

58 For instance, see S. L. de Lange and L. M. Mügge, 'Gender and right-wing populism in the Low Countries. Ideological variations across parties and time', *Patterns of Prejudice* 49(1–2) (2015), 61–80; B. Sauer, 'Demokratie, Volk und Geschlecht. Radikaler Rechtspopulismus in Europa', in K. Pühl and B. Sauer (eds), *Kapitalismuskritische Gesellschaftsanalyse. Queer-feministische Positionen* (Münster: Westfälisches Dampfboot, 2018), 178–195; Wodak, T*he politics of fear*; N. Spierings and A. Zaslove, 'Gendering the vote for populist radical-right parties', *Patterns of Prejudice* 49(1–2) (2015), 135–162; T. Akkerman, 'Gender and the radical right in Western Europe. A comparative analysis of policy agendas', *Patterns of Prejudice* 49:1–2 (2015), 37–60; M. Köttig, R. Bitzan, and A. Petö (eds), *Gender and far right politics in Europe* (Cham: Palgrave Macmillan, 2017).

59 See K. M. Blee, *Inside organized racism. Women in the hate movement* (Berkeley, CA; London: University of California Press, 2003); K. M. Blee, *Women of the Klan. Racism and gender in the 1920s* (Berkeley, CA; London: University of California Press, 2009); K. M. Blee, *Women of the right. Comparisons and interplay across borders* (University Park, PA: Pennsylvania State University Press, 2012); K. M. Blee, *Understanding racist activism. Theory, methods and research* (London; New York: Routledge, Taylor & Francis Group, 2018).

60 K. M. Blee, 'Becoming a racist. Women in contemporary Ku Klux Klan and neo-Nazi groups', *Gender & Society* 10 (2003), 680–702.

61 Quoted from C. Matthie, 'Wie sich Frauen vor Migranten-Gewalt schützen können', *Deutschland Kurier* (17 January 2018), URL: www.deutschland-kurier.org/wie-sich-frauen-vor-migranten-gew alt-schuetzen-koennen/ [Accessed 16 June 2019].

62 S. Ahmed, *The cultural politics of emotion* (New York: Routledge, 2004).

63 S. Harding and K. Stewart, 'Anxieties of influence. Conspiracy theory and therapeutic culture in millenial America', in H. G. West and T. Sanders (eds), *Transparency and conspiracy. Ethnographies of suspicion in the new world order* (Durham, NC: Duke University Press, 2003), 282.

64 V. Hambauer and A. Mays, 'Wer wählt die AfD?', *Zeitschrift für Vergleichende Politikwissenschaft* 1 (2017), 141.

65 See E. Harteveld, W. Van Der Brug, S. Dahlberg and A. Kokkonen, 'The gender gap in populist radical-right voting. Examining the demand side in Western and Eastern Europe', *Patterns of Prejudice* 49(1–2) (2015), 103; N. Spierings and A. Zaslove, 'Gendering the vote for populist radical-right parties', 157.

66 Interview with Ines Graf* in Suhl in November 2018.

67 Ibid.

68 M. Quent, *Deutschland rechts außen. Wie die Rechten nach der Macht greifen und wie wir sie stoppen können* (München: Piper, 2019), 248.

69 See K. Arzheimer and C. C. Berning, 'How the Alternative for Germany (AfD) and their voters veered to the radical right, 2013–2017', *Electoral Studies* 60(1–10) (2019), 1–10; M. A. Hansen and J. Olsen, 'Flesh of the same flesh: A study of voters for the Alternative for Germany (AfD) in the 2017 federal election', *German Politics* 28(1) (2019), 1–19.

NOTES TO CHAPTER 2: WOLF PACKS:
POGROMS, PILLORIES AND RIOTS

1 Parts of this chapter are developed in a longer article, 'Performing "resistance" – the far right's master narrative' in *The Journal of Culture* (1), 13–21, authored by Julia Leser, Florian Spissinger, Jamela Homeyer and Tobias Neidel.

2 A good overview of the events can be found in Quent, *Deutschland rechts außen*.

3 M. Frohnmaier, 'Wenn der Staat die Bürger nicht mehr schützen kann, gehen die Menschen auf die Straße und schützen sich selber. Ganz einfach! Heute ist es Bürgerpflicht, die todbringendendie "Messermigration" zu stoppen! Es hätte deinen Vater, Sohn oder Bruder treffen können!', *Twitter* (26 August 2018), URL: twitter. com/Frohnmaier_AfD/status/1033806135990644744 [Accessed 3 November 2019].

4 Pro Chemnitz is a non-profit organisation founded by the lawyer Martin Kohlmann in 2009. Martin Kohlmann has been active in the far-right scene for twenty years. In the summer of 2019, Pro Chemnitz was said to have had around thirty active members. None the less, it took part in the 2019 local elections and received 7.6 per cent of the votes and thus five of the sixty seats on the city council. On the occasion of the 2018 Chemnitz riots, some Pro Chemnitz protesters formed a vigilante group whose members were

Notes

later charged with forming a terrorist organisation and planning armed assaults on migrants and political adversaries (see S. Locke, '"Revolution Chemnitz": Eine selbsternannte Bürgerwehr', *FAZ* (1 October 2018), URL: www.faz.net/aktuell/politik/inland/revo lution-chemnitz-eine-selbsternannte-buergerwehr-15816565.html [Accessed 25 October 2019].

5 J. Gruntert, 'Der Abend, an dem der Rechtsstaat aufgab', *Zeit Online* (28 August 2018), URL: www.zeit.de/gesellschaft/zeit geschehen/2018–08/chemnitz-rechte-demonstration-ausschreitun gen-polizei [Accessed 3 November 2019].

6 C. Miller-Idriss, 'The United German extreme right', *Centre for Analysis of the Radical Right* (2018), URL: www.radicalrightanal ysis.com/2018/09/10/the-united-german-extreme-right/ [Accessed 25 June 2019].

7 J. Leser, F. Spissinger, J. Homeyer and T. Neidel, 'Performing "resistance" – the far right's master narrative', *The Journal of Culture* 8(1), 13–21; J. Leser and F. Spissinger, 'The functionality of affects. Conceptualizing far-right populist politics beyond negative emotions', *Global Discourse* 10(2), 325–342.

8 B. Manthe, 'Scenes of "civil" war? Radical right narratives on Chemnitz', *Centre for Analysis of the Radical Right* (2018), URL: www.radicalrightanalysis.com/2018/10/17/scenes-of-civil-war-ra dical-right-narratives-on-chemnitz/ [Accessed 25 June 2019].

9 D. Intelmann, 'Sieben Thesen zur urbanen Krise von Chemnitz', *sub/urban. Zeitschrift für kritische Stadtforschung* 7(1/2) (2019), 189–202.

10 H. Funke, 'Eine Minderheit, die zu allem fähig ist', *Süddeutsche Zeitung* (3 October 2018), URL: www.sueddeutsche.de/politik/che mnitz-eine-minderheit-die-zu-allem-faehig-ist-1.4154943 [Accessed 16 November 2019].

11 R. F. Inglehart and P. Norris, *Trump, Brexit, and the Rise of Populism. Economic Have-nots and Cultural Backlash*, Harvard Kennedy School. Faculty Research Working Paper Series RWP16-026 (August 2016); T. Schwarzbözl and M. Fatke, 'Außer Protesten nichts gewesen? Das politische Potenzial der AfD', *Politische Vierteljahresschrift* 57(2) (2016), 276–299, doi: 10.5771/0032–3470–2016–2-276.

12 C. von Braun, 'anti-Genderismus. Über das Feindbild Geschlechterforschung', *Kursbuch* 192 (2017), 28–45.

13 S. Wagenknecht, 'Wagenknecht lehnt offene Grenzen und Migrationspakt ab', *SWR* (30 November 2018), URL: www. swr.de/swraktuell/Linken-Fraktionschefin-im-SWR-Interview-Wa genknecht-lehnt-offene-Grenzen-und-Migrationspakt-ab,intervi

ew-d-woche-wagenknecht-100.html [Accessed 16 November 2019].

14 M. Ecke, 'What does Chemnitz tell us about the growth of right-wing radicalism in Germany?', *Social Europe* (2018), URL: www.socialeurope.eu/what-does-chemnitz-tell-us-about-the-growth-of-right-wing-radicalism-in-germany [Accessed 25 June 2019].

15 See D. Intelmann, 'Sieben Thesen zur urbanen Krise von Chemnitz', *sub/urban. Zeitschrift für kritische Stadtforschung* 7(1/2) (2019), 191; Miller-Idriss, 'The United German extreme right'.

16 Leser et al., 'Performing "resistance"', 16; see also Miller-Idriss, 'The United German extreme right'.

17 Miller-Idriss, 'The United German extreme right'.

18 For more information see J. Leser et al., 'Performing "resistance"', 16.

19 Leser et al., 'Performing "resistance"' 16.

20 C. Mudde, *The Far Right Today* (Cambridge; Medford: Polity Press, 2019), 32–38.

21 Archieved in B. von Bülow, *Bülow's 'Hammer and Anvil' Speech before the Reichstag* (11 December 1899), URL: wwi.lib.byu.edu/index.php/Bülow%27s_%27Hammer_and_Anvil%27_Speech_before_the_Reichstag [Accessed 3 November 2019].

22 Quoted from Der Flügel, *Kyffhäusertreffen 2018 – Rede von Björn Höcke* [Video file] (11 July 2018), URL: www.youtube.com/watch?v=kbLikMxEsqk [Accessed 17 May 2020].

23 J. Goebbels, 'Was wollen wir im Reichstag?', in H. S. van Berk (ed.), *Der Angriff, Aufsätze aus der Kampfzeit* (München: Franz Eher Nachfolger, 1935 [Reprint]), 71 and 73.

24 B. Sax, *Animals in the Third Reich. Pets, scapegoats and the Holocaust* (New York: Continuum, 2000).

25 A. Flack, 'Continental creatures. Animals in contemporary European history', *Contemporary European History* 27(3) (2018), https://doi.org/10.1017/S0960777318000036, 525.

26 M. Felton, *Guarding Hitler* (London: Pen and Sword, 2014), 123, quoted in Kølvraa, 'Wolves in sheep's clothing?', 113.

27 M. Fulbrook, 'The threat of the radical right in Germany', *Patterns of Prejudice* 28(3–4) (1994), 57–66, 58.

28 C. Wowtscherk, *Was wird, wenn die Zeitbombe hochgeht? Eine sozialgeschichtliche Analyse der fremdenfeindlichen Ausschreitungen in Hoyerswerda im September 1991* (Göttingen: V & R Unipress, 2014), 216.

29 Ibid., 178.

30 P. Panayi, 'Racial violence in the new Germany 1990–93', *Contemporary European History* 3(3) (1994), 265–287.

Notes

31 Wowtscherk, *Was wird, wenn die Zeitbombe hochgeht?*, 247.
32 According to Fulbrook, 'The threat of the radical right in Germany', 59: 'In 1991, 14.1 per cent of infringements of law were anti-Semitic in character: eighty-four cases of desecration of Jewish cemeteries, synagogues, buildings, memorials. Of forty cases of desecration of cemeteries, five were in East Germany, thirty-five in West Germany.'
33 Ibid., 59.
34 Ibid., 61.
35 Ibid., 62.
36 R. Erices, 'Hetzjagd im Augst 1975 in Erfurt. Wie Ausländerfeindlichkeit in der DDR verharmlost und verleugnet wurde', *Gerbergasse 18. Thüringer Vierteljahreszeitschrift für Zeitgeschichte und Politik* 89(4) (2018), 22–25.
37 G. Wiegel, 'Rechte Erlebniswelten', in M. Dust, L. Lohmann and G. Steffens (eds), *Events and Edutainment. Jahrbuch für Pädagogik 2016* (Frankfurt am Main: Peter Lang, 2016), 95–106, 97.
38 S. Aust and D. Laabs, *Heimatschutz. Der Staat und die Mordserie des NSU* (München: Pantheon, 2014).
39 D. Begrich, '"Wir sind das Pack". Von Hoyerswerda nach Heidenau', *Blätter für deutsche und internationale Politik* 60(10) (2015), 10.
40 H. Kleffner and A. Spangenberg (eds), *Generation Hoyerswerda. Das Netzwerk militanter Neonazis in Brandenburg* (Berlin-Brandenburg: Be.bra Verlag, 2016).
41 Antifa in Leipzig, 'Colditz: Neonazi mit Crystal Meth aufgegriffen', *Inventati* (14 October 2014), URL: www.inventati.org/leipzig/?p=2513 [Accessed 2 November 2019].
42 T. Datt, 'Flucht aus Colditz. Eine rechtsfreie Zone im mittelsächsischen Hügelland', in H. Kleffner, M. Meisner, C. Ditsch and K. Stuttmann (eds), *Unter Sachsen: Zwischen Wut und Willkommen* (Berlin: Ch. Links Verlag, 2017), 211–225.
43 Ibid., 213–217.
44 The long tradition of violence in Eastern Germany, especially in the 1990s, has been taken up and documented under the hashtag 'The years of the baseball bats' (*Baseballschlägerjahre*) on twitter. See also: ZDF, '#Baseballschlägerjahre' [Video file] (2 November 2019), URL: www.zdf.de/nachrichten/heute-plus/videos/baseballschlaegerjahre-rechte-gewalt-neonazis-100.html [Accessed 3 November 2019]. There are also several accounts of the 1990s in the East in novels and prize-winning factual accounts: M. Präkels, *Als ich mit Hitler Schnapskirsche aß* (Berlin: Verbrecher

Notes

Verlag, 2017); D. Schulz, 'Wir waren wie Brüder. Jugendliche in Ostdeutschland', *FAZ* (1 October 2018), URL: www.taz.de/ Jugendliche-in-Ostdeutschland/!5536453/ [Accessed 3 November 2019]; E. Dieschereit, *Blumen für Otello. Über die Verbrechen von Jena* (Berlin: Secession Verlag, 2014); L. Rietzschel, *Mit der Faust in die Welt schlagen* (Berlin: Ullstein Verlag, 2018).

45 This quote and the following are taken from R. Gebhardt, 'Hauptfeind Liberalismus', *Magazin 'der rechte rand' Ausgabe 173 – Juli/August 2018* (2018), URL: www.der-rechterand. de/ archive/3461/thor-von-waldstein-liberalismus/ [Accessed 17 May 2020].

46 R. Gebhardt, 'Hauptfeind Liberalismus', *Magazin 'der rechte rand' Ausgabe 173 – Juli/August 2018* (2018), URL: www.der-rechte-rand.de/archive/3461/thor-von-waldstein-liberalismus/ [Accessed 17 May 2020].

47 Bundesamt für Justiz, *Basic Law for the Federal Republic of Germany* (28 March 2019), URL: www.gesetze-im-internet.de/ englisch_gg/englisch_gg.html#p0111 [Accessed 3 November 2019].

48 With the exception of Vietnamese contract workers.

49 C. Fuchs and P. Middelhoff, *Das Netzwerk der neuen Rechten. Wer sie lenkt, wer sie finanziert und wie sie die Gesellschaft verändern* (Reinbek bei Hamburg: Rowohlt, 2019), 122.

50 This and the following statements by Björn Höcke have been transcribed and translated from Für Gerechtigkeit (6 July 2019). *Grandiose Rede von Björn Höcke, AfD. Flügeltreffen in Leinefelde (TH) 06.07.2019* [Video file] Retrieved from www.youtube.com/ watch?v=gX08pRXNEEU.

51 Quent, *Deutschland rechts außen*, 231.

52 R. Pates and M. Schochow (eds), *Der 'Ossi'. Mikropolitische Studien über einen symbolischen Ausländer* (Wiesbaden: Springer VS, 2013).

53 Interview with Michael Schneider*, member of THÜGIDA, in Leipzig, November 2018.

54 Jörg Urban on 18 March 2019, during the AfD event *Heimat Saxony* in Grosspösna.

55 M. Kleine-Hartlage, 'Der entfesselte Westen: Islam und der Tumor des Liberalismus', *Compact – Magazin für Souveränität* 2017(5) (2017), 38–39.

56 Ibid., 38.

57 Ibid., 39.

58 M. Müller-Mertens, '"Dass ein gutes Deutschland blühe": Das patriotische Erbe der SED', *Compact – Magazin für Souveränität* 2017(5) (2017), 20–21.

Notes

59 B. Brecht, 'Children's Hymn' (1950), *Wikipedia*, URL: https:// en.wikipedia.org/wiki/Children%27s_Hymn [Accessed 17 May 2020].

60 M. Müller-Mertens, 'Deutsche demokratische Reserve: Bürgerprotest zwischen Elbe und Oder', *Compact – Magazin für Souveränität* 2017(5) (2017), 14–16.

61 Spiegel Online, *Der Spiegel 36/2015 – Inhaltsverzeichnis* (29 August 2015), URL: www.spiegel.de/spiegel/print/index-2015-36. html [Accessed 4 November 2019].

62 On 20 August 2015, *DIE ZEIT* journalist Stefan Schirmer proposed a 'Säxit' in order to 'protect' the rest of Germany from Saxony's alleged problem with right-wing extremism. See S. Schirmer, 'Dann geht doch! Hass, Extremismus und Abschottung in Sachsen: Ist es Zeit für einen Säxit?' URL: https://www.zeit.de/2015/34/sachsen-austritt-bundesrepublik-rechtsextremismus-pegida [Accessed 4 April 2020]. The article caused an uproar. On 28 August 2015, AfD politician Sebastian Wippel took up the idea of a 'Säxit' on his blog and gave it a positive spin: 'A separate Saxon state – but gladly! Ultimately, this would mean that almost all AfD demands would have to be implemented automatically'. See S. Wippel, 'Warum der Säxit eine gute Idee ist', URL: https://www.sebastian-wippel.de/ index.php/warum-der-saexit-eine-gute-idee- ist/ [Accessed 4 April 2020]. On 12 October 2015, PEDIGA organiser Tatjana Festerling demanded the 'Säxit' and Saxoy's sovereignty during her speech at a PEGIDA demonstration in Dresden, saying 'The Saxon people have the right to statehood.' See ARD, 'Schlegl in Aktion: Privater Säxit' [Video file] (21 March 2020), URL: https://www.daserste.de/ unterhaltung/comedy-satire/extra-3/videosextern/schlegl-in-aktion-privater-saexit-102.html [Accessed 4 April 2020]. On 6 September 2018, far-right magazine *Compact* published an article taking up the idea of a 'Säxit'. See *Compact* Magazine, '"Nu, macht doch Euern Dreck alleene" – Die Idee eines "Säxits" gewinnt an Zuspruch', URL: https://www.compact-online.de/nu-macht-doch-euern-dreck-alleene-die-idee-eines-saexits-gewinnt-an-zuspru ch/ [Accessed 4 April 2020].

63 See D. Kuhn, 'Unsere andere Fahne', *Politically Incorrect* (25 November 2012), URL: www.pi-news.net/2011/09/unsere-andere-fahne/ [Accessed 16 November 2019].

64 D. Meiering, A. Dziri, N. Foroutan, S. Teune, E. Lehnert and M. Abou Taam, *Brückennarrative. Verbindende Elemente in der Radikalisierung von Gruppen* (Frankfurt am Main: Leibniz-Institut Hessische Stiftung Friedens- und Konfliktforschung, 2018), 22–25.

Notes

65 wahlrecht.de, 'Stimmenanteile der AfD bei den jeweils letzten Landtagswahlen in den Bundesländern bis Oktober 2019' [Graph], *Statista* (27 October 2019), URL: de.statista.com/statistik/daten/studie/320946/umfrage/ergebnisse-der-afd-bei-den-landtagswahlen/ [Accessed 17 May 2020].

66 Focus Online, *Strafanzeige gegen Gauland wegen Verdachts auf Volksverhetzung* (6 June 2018), URL: www.focus.de/politik/deutschland/vogelschiss-aeusserung-strafanzeige-gegen-gauland-wegen-verdachts-auf-volksverhetzung_id_9049620.html [Accessed 4 November 2019]; M. Wehner and E. Lohse, '"Nicht als Nachbarn": Gauland beleidigt Boateng', *FAZ* (29 May 2016), URL: www.faz.net/aktuell/politik/inland/afd-vize-gauland-beleid igt-jerome-boateng-14257743.html [Accessed 4 November 2019]; Welt, *Einstweilige Verfügung gegen AfD-Politiker Maier* (10 January 2018), URL: www.welt.de/politik/deutschland/art icle172355288/Halbneger-Gericht-erlaesst-Verfuegung-gegen-AfD-Mann-Maier.html [Accessed 4 November 2019]; S. Leber, 'Rechte vor Einzug in den Bundestag. So extrem sind die Kandidaten der AfD', *Tagesspiegel* (21 September 2017), URL: www.tagesspiegel.de/themen/reportage/rechte-vor-einzug-in-den-bundestag-so-extr em-sind-die-kandidaten-der-afd/20350578.html [Accessed 4 November 2019]. On conspiracy theories, see M. Butter, *Nichts ist, wie es scheint. Über Verschwörungstheorien* (Berlin: Suhrkamp, 2018).

67 S. Lübbe, 'Junge AfD-Wähler: Überzeugungswähler', *Zeit Campus* (1 November 2019), URL: www.zeit.de/campus/2019-10/junge-afd-waehler-erfurt-thueringen-landtagswahl [Accessed 4 November 2019].

68 O. Niedermayer and J. Hofrichter, 'Die Wählerschaft der AfD. Wer ist sie, woher kommt sie und wie weit rechts steht sie?', *ZParl Zeitschrift für Parlamentsfragen* 47(2) (2016), 267–285.

69 These interviews were conducted by the authors with several research assistants (Philipp Lemmerich, Jamela Homeyer, Mario Futh) in the context of our research funded by the Federal Ministry of Research and Education in 2018 and 2019 in Saxony, Thuringia, Berlin and Schleswig-Holstein. For the development of some of these research results in the UK context, see S. Valluvan, 'Defining and challenging the new nationalism', *Juncture* 23:4 (2017), 232–239.

70 Cramer, *The politics of resentment*.

71 Patzelt, 'Mängel in der Responsivität oder Störungen in der Kommunikation?'.

72 A. Przybyszewski, 'Ex Oriente Lux', *Sezession* 90 (June 2019), 7.

Notes

73 G. Kubitschek, 'Sachsen', *Sezession* 90 (June 2019), 1.
74 G. Pickel, 'Eine sächsische politische Kultur des Extremismus?', in G. Pickel and O. Decker (eds), *Extremismus in Sachsen. Eine kritische Bestandsaufnahme* (Leipzig: Edition Leipzig, 2016), 18.
75 J. Seidel, 'Warum Sachsen? Warum der Osten?', *Sezession* 90 (June 2019), 18.
76 See Richter, *Hört endlich zu!*.
77 M. Minkenberg, *The radical right in Eastern Europe: Democracy under siege?* (New York: Palgrave Macmillan, 2017).
78 Ibid, 145.
79 Ibid., 144.
80 See *Compact*, '"Nu, macht doch Euern Dreck alleene" – Die Idee eines "Säxits" gewinnt an Zuspruch', URL: https://www.comp act-online.de/nu-macht-doch-euern-dreck-alleene-die-idee-eines-sa exits-gewinnt-an-zuspruch/ [Accessed 4 April 2020].
81 Ibid.
82 I. Ayata, 'Deutschland liegt in Sachsen', in H. Kleffner, M. Meisner, C. Ditsch and K. Stuttmann (eds), *Unter Sachsen: Zwischen Wut und Willkommen* (Berlin: Ch. Links Verlag, 2017), 260.
83 Quent, *Deutschland rechts außen*, 231, 236, 24.
84 Ayata, 'Deutschland liegt in Sachsen', 261.

Notes to Chapter 3: Renaturing and the politics of *Heimat*

1 Quoted from S. Cagle, '"Bees, not refugees". The environmentalist roots of anti-immigrant bigotry', *The Guardian* (16 August 2019), URL: www.theguardian.com/environment/2019/aug/15/anti [Accessed 4 November 2019].
2 Federal Government Commissioner for the New Federal States, *Annual Report of the Federal Government on the Status of German Unity 2018* (Berlin: Federal Ministry for Economic Affairs and Energy, 2018), 69.
3 THÜGIDA – short for Thuringia against the Islamicisation of the Occident – is a radical little relation of PEGIDA. It was a club focusing its political interest on migration and refugee rights. It consisted of a handful of members, most of them unabashedly *völkisch* and sceptical of the legitimacy of the German state. As far as we know, THÜGIDA has ceased operations since our interview.
4 Interview with Michael Schneider*, member of THÜGIDA in Leipzig, November 2018.
5 B. Forchtner, 'Nation, nature, purity. Extreme-right biodiversity in Germany', *Patterns of Prejudice* 53(3) (2019), 285–301, doi: 10.1080/0031322X.2019.1592303, 2–3.

Notes

6   N. Franke, 'Rechtsextremismus und Ökolandbau. Ganzheitlich und organisch mit braunem Anstrich', *Ökologie und Landbau* 165, 2013(1), 50.

7   *Hier & Jetzt* 2013, quoted in A. Schmidt, *Völkische Siedler/innen im ländlichen Raum* (Berlin: Amadeu Antonio Stiftung, n.d.), 7.

8   These journalists have built their careers on warning the public of the rural far-right scene. Their most recent book *Völkische Landnahme* is the subject of a range of lawsuits, as many people who settled in the countryside see themselves as conservative, not as neo-Nazis, and it is currently not in print.

9   See, for example, A. Hennings, 'Kampf um die Matten – Wie die rechte Szene den Kampfsport instrumentalisiert', *Deutschlandfunk* (17 March 2019), URL: www.deutschlandfun kkultur.de/kampf-um-die-matten-wie-die-rechte-szene-den-kampf sport.966.de.html?dram:article_id=443785 [Accessed 4 November 2019].

10   See, for example, A. Lanzke, 'Grüne Tarnfarbe. Rechtsextremismus unter dem Deckmantel des Umweltschutzes', *Belltower News* (7 November 2012), URL: www.belltower.news/gruene-tarnfa rbe-rechtsextremismus-unter-dem-deckmantel-des-umweltschut zes-35444/ [Accessed 16 November 2019].

11   Forchtner, 'Nation, nature, purity', 5.

12   Umwelt & Aktiv, *Das Magazin für gesamtheitliches Denken: Umweltschutz, Tierschutz, Heimatschutz.* (n.d), URL: www. umweltundaktiv.de [Accessed 5 November 2019].

13   Quoted in A. Röpke and A. Speit, *Völkische Landnahme. Alte Sippen, junge Siedler, rechte Ökos* (Berlin: Links, 2019), 136.

14   Quoted from W. Megre, 'love productions', *Anastasia Website* (2019), URL: www.loveproductions.org/deutsch/raum-der-liebe/ [Accessed 16 November 2019].

15   See Anastasia Foundation, 'What is a family estate?', URL: https:// anastasia.ru/news/detail/1753/ [Accessed 7 April 2020].

16   For example, W. Megre, *Anastasia. Tochter der Taiga*, trans. H. Kunkel (Zürich: Govinda Verlag, 2003). More books have been published in German translation between 2003 and 2011.

17   Interview quotes in A. Rosga, *Anastasia-Bewegung – ein (un-) politisches Siedlungskonzept? Qualitative Feldforschung zu den Hintergründen und gesellschaftspolitischen Einstellungen inner-halb der Anastasia-Bewegung* (2018), 24 and 28.

18   See Bundestag, *Drucksache 19/7541* (Berlin: Bundestag, 2019).

19   Interview quotes in Rosga, *Anastasia-Bewegung*, 34. A contro-versial article in the environmental magazine *OYA* repeats both

Notes

the claims that Anastasia followers are right-wing and anti-Semitic, and the claims of the followers that such statements are widely cited but unrepresentative for the movement. See: A. Vetter, A. Humburg and L. Mallien, 'Anastasia – die Macht eines Phantoms', *OYA* 45 (2017), URL: http://oya-online.de/arti cle/read/2777-anastasia_die_macht_eines_phantoms.html?omit_overlay=59fa8b5371da6 [Accessed 5 November 2019].

20 See, for example, Urahnenerbe Germania, *Urahnenerbe Germania: Willkommen* (n.d.), URL: www.urahnenerbe.de [Accessed 5 November 2019].

21 B. Höcke and S. Hennig, *Nie zweimal in denselben Fluss* (Lüdinghausen: Manuscriptum, 2018), 253.

22 J. Davey and J. Ebner, 'The Great Replacement'. *The violent consequences of mainstreamed extremism* (London: Institute for Strategic Dialogue, 2019), 4.

23 This quote and the following are from the interview with Frank Michelchen*, farmer and founder of the initiative 'Wolf-free zones', in Leibsch (Brandenburg) in August 2019. Pauline Betche conducted the interview.

24 Cramer, *The politics of resentment*, 31.

25 Interview with Frank Michelchen.

26 Cramer, *The politics of resentment*, 32–33.

27 This quote and the following are from the interview with Thomas Frieder*, hunter, in Leipzig in November 2019. Pauline Betche conducted this interview.

28 See: S. Mau, *Transnationale Vergesellschaftung. Die Entgrenzung sozialer Lebenswelten.* (Frankfurt am Main; New York: Campus, 2007); P. A. Berger and A. Weiß, *Transnationalisierung sozialer Ungleichheit* (Wiesbaden: Springer VS, 2008), doi: 10.1007/978-3-531-91160-1; V. Weiß, *Die autoritäre Revolte. Die Neue Rechte und der Untergang des Abendlandes* (Stuttgart: Klett-Cotta, 2017).

29 Interview with Stephan Kaasche, volunteer at the Contact Office Wolves in Saxony, in Hoyerswerda in February 2019.

30 Forchtner, 'Nation, nature, purity', 2.

31 Schmidt, *Völkische Siedler/innen im ländlichen Raum*, 19.

32 J. Olsen, 'The perils of rootedness. On bioregionalism and right wing ecology in Germany', *Landscape Journal* 19(1–2) (2000), 73.

33 See B. Swan, 'Inside Virginia's creep white-power wolf cult', *Daily Beast* (13 April 2017), URL: www.thedailybeast.com/inside-virginias-creepy-white-power-wolf-cult [Accessed 5 November 2019].

34 During his visit to Germany in 2017, Jack Donovan was invited to speak at the Institut für Staatspolitik. Under the title

Notes

'Violence is golden', Donovan's speech on 18 February 2017 revolved around the topics of a 'culture of masculinity' and the return to 'tribal thinking'. His speech was recorded, the video being available online: kanal schnellroda, *Violence Is Golden – Jack Donovan beim IfS* [Video file] (13 March 2017), URL: www.youtube.com/watch?v=4v48H9FreyY [Accessed 3 November 2019].

35 D. Zuckerberg, *Not all dead white men. Classics and misogyny in the digital age.* (Cambridge, MA: Harvard University Press, 2018), 12.

36 J. Donovan, *The Way of Men* [E-book edition] (Milwaukee: Dissonant Hum, 2012). This book has been published in German translation by Kubitschek's own New Right publishing house Antaios.

37 Ibid.

38 Ibid.

39 Quotations from kanal schnellroda, *Violence Is Golden – Jack Donovan beim IfS.*

40 B. Forchtner and Ö. Özvatan, 'Beyond the "German Forest": Environmental communication by the far right in Germany', in B. Forchtner (ed.), *The far right and the environment* (Abingdon; New York: Routledge, 2019), 217–220.

41 For example, F. Hartlieb, *Einsame Wölfe* (Hamburg: Hoffmann und Campe Verlag, 2018).

Notes to Chapter 4: Herding wayward citiens

1 Quotation from a speech by Björn Höcke for the Junge Alternative (Young Alternatives), the AfD's youth organisation, in Dresden on 17 January 2017, quoted from the report on the AfD by the Federal Office for the Protection of the Constitution (Verfassungsschutz, VS), available online: A. Meister, A. Biselli and M. Reuter, 'Wir veröffentlichen das Verfassungsschutz-Gutachten zur AfD', *Netzpolitik.org* (28 January 2019), URL: https://netzpolitik.org/2019/wir-veroeffentlichen-das-verfassungsschutz-gutachten-zur-afd/#2019–01–15_BfV-AfD-Gutachten_Quelle-265 [Accessed 14 November 2019].

2 Discussion 'Elections 2019 – Do we have a choice?' on 7 November 2019 at Leipzig University.

3 C. Mudde, *On extremism and democracy in Europe* (London; New York: Routledge, 2016).

4 For example, F. Decker, 'The "Alternative for Germany"': Factors behind its emergence and profile of a new right-wing populist

Notes

party', *German Politics and Society* 34(2) (2016), 1–16; K. Grabow, 'PEGIDA and the Alternative für Deutschland. Two sides of the same coin?', *European View* 15(2) (2016), 173–181; Ö. Özvatan and B. Forchtner, 'The far-right Alternative für Deutschland in Germany: Towards a "happy ending"?', in A. Waring (ed.), *The new authoritarianism: Vol. 2: A risk analysis of the European alt-right phenomenon* (Stuttgart: ibidem, 2019), 199–226; J. Schwörer, 'Alternative für Deutschland. From the streets to the Parliament?', in M. Caiani and O. Císař (eds), *Radical right movement parties in Europe* (Abingdon; New York: Routledge, 2019), 29–45.

5 About €40.5 million in 2015, €50 million in 2016, €104 million in 2017, €120 million in 2018, but in 2019 reduced to €115 million. The dramatic increase in funding does not fortuitously coincide with the voting results for the AfD: it is meant to prevent their increase.

6 We summarised these hypotheses in Dellenbaugh-Losse, Homeyer, Leser and Pates, 'Toxische Orte?', 2020, 47–82.

7 For example, Arzheimer and Berning, 'How the Alternative for Germany (AfD) and their voters veered to the radical right'; Hansen and Olsen, 'Flesh of the same flesh'.

8 For example, M. Minkenberg, *Die neue radikale Rechte im Vergleich* (Opladen: Westdeutscher Verlag, 1998); J. J. Rosellini, *The German new right* (London: Hurst Publishers, 2019); R. Woods, *Germany's new right as culture and politics* (Basingstoke and New York: Palgrave Macmillan, 2007).

9 This is the title of Nitzan Shoshan's excellent case study on Germany's attempt to domesticate indigenous and potentially hazardous nationalism.

10 H. Pilkington, *Loud and proud. Passion and politics in the English Defence League* (Manchester University Press, 2016).

11 All subsequent quotations come from our interview with Katharina Schulte* and Michael Schneider* in Leipzig in November 2018.

12 THÜGIDA is waning but turned into the far-right organisation A Nation Helps Itself (Ein Volk hilft sich selbst).

13 The non-profit organisation is being observed by three regional Offices for the Protection of the Constitution as a potentially dangerous right-wing organisation. Its Facebook page had 8,857 followers in 2019.

14 N. Shoshan, *The management of hate* (Princeton: Princeton University Press, 2016), 89.

15 Ibid., 79.

16 Ibid., 200.

17 Ibid., 171.

Notes

18 What the 'extreme right danger' is (for the political and the legal system) and how one recognises it is negotiated in a discursive way, as we have shown elsewhere: R. Pates, 'Die Hölle sind immer die anderen. Moralische Ordnungen in Trainings gegen "Rechtsextremisten"', in FKR (ed.), *Ordnung. Macht. Extremismus* (Wiesbaden: VS Verlag für Sozialwissenschaften, 2011), 212–239; D. Schmidt, R. Pates and S. Karawanskij, 'Verwaltung politischer Devianz', in FKR (ed.), *Ordnung. Macht. Extremismus* (Wiesbaden: VS Verlag für Sozialwissenschaften, 2011), 194–196.

19 Shoshan, *The management of hate*, 223.

20 Ibid., 225.

21 Ibid., 211.

22 Ibid., 208.

23 Fulbrook, *The threat of the radical right in Germany*, 63.

24 M. Czollek, *Desintegriert euch!* (München: Carl Hanser Verlag, 2018), 35. This immunisation thesis is quite prevalent, thanks to Pauline Betche for pointing this out. So for instance, the Saxon Prime Minister Kurt Biedenkopf (1990–2002) claimed in a much-quoted interview to the *Sächsische Zeitung* on 28 September 2000, despite all the evidence to the contrary: 'In Saxony, no houses have been burnt, no one has died [...] And the Saxon population has proved itself totally immune in the face of right-wing extremist temptations', quoted in M. Jennerjahn, 'Programme und Projekte gegen Rechtsextremismus vor Ort – Das Fallbeispiel Sachsen', in S. Braun, A. Geisler and M. Gerster (eds), *Strategien der extremen Rechten. Hintergründe, Analysen, Antworten* (Wiesbaden: Springer VS, 2016); see also Leser and Spissinger, 'The functionality of affects'.

25 Wodak, *The politics of fear*; R. Wodak, 'Entering the "post-shame era"', *Global Discourse* 9 (2019), 195–213.

26 See G. Maier, 'Thüringens Innenminister Maier zur rechten Unterwanderung. "Die Gleichgültigkeit ist das eigentliche Gift"', *Deutschlandfunk* (5 October 2020), URL: www.deutschlandfunk.de/ thueringens-innenminister-maier-zur-rechten-unterwanderung.694. de.html?dram:article_id=460373 [Accessed 14 November 2019].

27 See also the dramatisation of racist and minority violence in a number of new novels with autobiographical traits: Rietzschel, *Mit der Faust in die Welt schlagen*; Präkels, *Als ich mit Hitler Schnapskirschen aß*; I. Geipel, *Umkämpfte Zone. Mein Bruder, der Osten und der Hass* (Stuttgart: Clett-Kotta, 2019).

28 Tagesschau, Halbjahresbilanz 2019. Bereits mehr als 8600 rechte Straftaten (14 August 2020), URL: www.tagesschau.de/

Notes

inland/kriminalitaet-rechtsextremismus-101.html?fbclid=IwAR
22YH73Ree-rYTMZRGdNRspWYRS4hGSVLQGvGX3tdaKbHVB
FRO61XgISSk [Accessed 17 May 2020].

29 Shoshan, *The management of hate*, 13.

30 D. Ellerbrock, L. Koch, S. Müller-Mall, M. Münkler, J. Scharloth, D. Schrage and G. Schwerhoff, 'Invektivität – Perspektiven eines neuen Forschungsprogramms in den Kultur- und Sozial-wissenschaften', *Kulturwissenschaftliche Zeitschrift* 2 (2017), 2.

31 I. Hacking, *The social construction of what?* (Cambridge, MA: Harvard University Press, 1999).

32 D. Caramani and L. Manucci, 'National past and populism', *West European Politics* 42 (2019), 1178.

33 For example, F. Decker, 'Germany: right-wing populist failures and left-wing successes', in D. Albertazzi and D. McDonnell (eds), *Twenty-first century populism* (Basingstoke: Palgrave, 2008), 119–134.

34 Interview with Claudia Dreichsel* and Christian Koch* in Freiburg, December 2019. The interview was conducted by Ronja Morgenthaler.

35 R. Ogman, *Against the Nation* (Porsgrunn: New Compass Press, 2013).

36 I. Erdem, 'Anti-deutsche Linke oder anti-linke Deutsche? Eine sachliche Betrachtung.', *UTOPIE kreativ* 192 (October 2006), 926–939. Thanks to Pauline Betche for pointing this out.

37 Interview with Thomas Ebermann in Berlin in December 2018. The interview was conducted by Ronja Morgenthaler.

38 Czollek, *Desintegriert euch.*

39 Interview with Thorsten Mense in Leipzig in November 2018. The interview was conducted by Ronja Morgenthaler.

40 All quotations in this paragraph are taken from an interview with the members of a local memorial site association in Gera in July 2018.

Notes to Chapter 5: Affective politics

1 Parts of this chapter are developed in 'The functionality of affects. Conceptualizing far-right populist politics beyond negative emotions' in *Global Discourse* 10(2), 325–342, by Julia Leser and Florian Spissinger.

2 Quoted from C. van Laak, 'Gefühlte Realität. AfD-Wahlkampf im Berlin', *Deutschlandfunk.* (14 September 2019), URL: www.deutschlandfunk.de/afd-wahlkampf-in-berlin-gefuehlte-realitaet.1773.de.html?dram:article_id=365806 [Accessed 2 October 2019].

Notes

3 Stephan Kaasche in a public communication during a wolf tour in and around Rietschen, 17 August 2019.

4 See, for example, M. Haselrieder, and J. Bartz, 'Mit der Angst auf Stimmenfang. Der Wolf im Wahlkampf der AfD in Sachsen', ZDF (20 August 2019), URL: www.zdf.de/nachrichten/heute/mit-der-angst-auf-stimmenfang-der-wolf-im-wahlkampf-der-afd-100.html [Accessed 17 May 2020].

5 Cramer, The politics of resentment.

6 Interview on 8 November 2018 with Stephan Locke, correspondent for the Frankfurter Allgemeine Zeitung in Saxony, for the BBC programme The Wolves Are Coming Back.

7 The numbers cited and the figure are provided by the Federal Documentation and Information Centre on the Topic Wolf, see DBBW, Dokumentations- und Beratungsstelle des Bundes zum Thema Wolf (2019) URL: www.dbb-wolf.de/ [Accessed 16 November 2019].

8 See B. Knapstein, 'Erstmals Wolfsjagd auf Pferde beobachtet', Böhme-Zeitung (22 May 2018), URL: western-journal.de/ 2018/05/22/boehme-zeitung-18-mai-2018-erstmals-wolfsjagd-auf-pferde-beobachtet/ [Accessed 16 November 2019]; Deutscher Jagdverband, Achtung Falschmeldung! (29 May 2018), URL: www.jagdverband.de/content/achtung-falschmeldung [Accessed 16 November 2019].

9 C. Powell, 'What the PM learnt about the Germans', in H. James and M. Stone (eds), When the Wall came down. Reactions to German unification. (New York; London: Routledge, 1992), 234, emphasis in original. Powell's memorandum of the Prime Minister's meeting at Chequers in 1990 was leaked to The Independent on Sunday and the German newspaper Der Spiegel and published in 1992 in this anthology.

10 A. Schildt, '"German Angst". Überlegungen zur Mentalitätsgeschichte der Bundesrepublik', in D. Münkel and J. Schwarzkopf (ed.), Geschichte als Experiment. Studien zu Politik, Kultur und Alltag im 19. und 20. Jahrhundert (Frankfurt am Main: Campus Verlag, 2004), 87–97.

11 S. Ahmed, The cultural politics of emotion (Edinburgh: Edinburgh University Press, 2014), 72.

12 Ibid., 4. See also T. Brennan, The transmission of affect (Ithaca: Cornell University Press, 2004).

13 Ahmed, The cultural politics of emotion, 117 and 119.

14 Ibid., 119.

15 Anonymous author, Völkischer Aufklärer. Informationen für das deutsche Volk! (2019); see Völkischer Aufklärer, 'Die Wölfe

Notes

im Schafspelz oder die fast perfekte Täuschung', *Blogeintrag in Völkischer Aufklärer. Informationen für das deutsche Volk!* (16 February 2019), URL: www.voelkischer-aufklaerer.de/2019/02/16/die-woelfe-im-schafspelz-oder-die-fast-perfekte-taeuschung/ [Accessed 5 November 2019]. The headline to this blog post is 'Wolves in sheep's clothing, or the almost perfect deception' (*Die Wölfe im Schafspelz oder die fast perfekte Täuschung*), and its anonymous author blames the Greens not only for politics driven by fear but for being a 'cancer eating away the German people', finishing the post with: 'Let's remove the cancer from the German people. Germany, wake up! Germany, rise up!'

16 D. Ellerbrock, et al., 'Invektivität', 5.

17 For example, Wodak, *The politics of fear.*

18 For example, M. Cox and M. Durham, 'The politics of anger', in P. Hainsworth (ed.), *Politics of the extreme right. From the margins to the mainstream* (London: Bloomsbury, 2000), 287–311; J. Ebner, *The rage. The vicious circle of Islamist and far-right extremism* (London: I. B. Tauris & Co. Ltd, 2017); P. Mishra, *Age of anger. A history of the present.* (London: Allen Lane, 2017); C. Koppetsch, *Die Gesellschaft des Zorns. Rechtspopulismus im globalen Zeitalter* (Bielefeld: transcript, 2019).

19 For example, Blee, *Inside organised racism*; C. Emcke, *Against hate* (Cambridge: Polity Press, 2019); J. Garland and J. Treadwell, 'The new politics of hate? An assessment of the appeal of the English Defence League amongst disadvantaged white working-class communities in England', *Journal of Hate Studies* 10 (2012), 123–142.

20 Leser and Spissinger, 'The functionality of affects', 326.

21 V. L. Henderson, 'Is there hope for anger? The politics of spatial-izing and (re)producing an emotion', *Emotion, Space and Society* 1 (2008), 29.

22 S. Ngai, *Ugly feelings* (Cambridge, MA: Harvard University Press, 2007), 5.

23 See Leser and Spissinger, 'The functionality of affects', 326.

24 M. Billig, *Banal nationalism* (London: Sage, 1995), 7.

25 See Leser and Spissinger, 'The functionality of affects', 327.

26 J. Busher, P. Giurlando and G. B. Sullivan, 'Introduction. The emotional dynamics of backlash politics beyond anger, hate, fear, pride, and loss', *Humanity & Society* 42 (2018), 402.

27 For example, J. Habermas, *Faktizität und Geltung* (Frankfurt am Main: Suhrkamp, 1998), and J. Rawls, *Political liberalism* (New York: Columbia University Press, 1996).

Notes

28 See Leser and Spissinger, 'The functionality of affects', 328.
29 See J. Bender and R. Bingener, 'Marc Jongen. Parteiphilosoph der AfD', *FAZ* (15 January 2016), URL: www.faz.net/aktuell/politik/inland/marc-jongen-ist-afd-politiker-und-philosoph-14005731.html [Accessed 16 November 2019].
30 See Leser and Spissinger, 'The functionality of affects', 325–342; Leser et al., 'Performing "resistance"', 13–21.
31 Leser and Spissinger, 'The functionality of affects', 328.
32 See M. Jongen, 'Der Parteiphilosoph der AfD', *Frankfurter Allgemeine* (15 January 2016), URL: www.faz.net/aktuell/politik/inland/marc-jongen-ist-afd-politiker-und-philosoph-14005731.html [Accessed 1 February 2021].
33 See Leser et al., 'Performing "resistance"', 13–21.
34 Leser et al., 'Performing "resistance"', 17.
35 R. Bromley, 'The politics of displacement. The Far Right narrative of Europe and its "others"', *From the European South* 3 (2018), 13.
36 See Leser et al., 'Performing "resistance"', 17.
37 J. Bruner, 'The narrative construction of reality', *Critical Inquiry* 18 (1991), 4. See also P. Ewing and S. S. Silbey, 'Subversive stories and hegemonic tales. Toward a sociology of narrative', *Law and Society Review* 29 (1995): 197–226; M. Somers, 'The narrative constitution of identity. A relational and network approach', *Theory and Society* 2 (1994): 605–649.
38 Brauer, 'Bowling mit Wölfen', 47.
39 Thanks to Pauline Betche for this observation.
40 The interview was conducted by Mario Futh, and we are grateful to Melissa Steinbach for having facilitated the meetings.
41 Leser and Spissinger, 'The functionality of affects', 332.
42 Ibid.
43 Shoshan, *The management of hate*; Blee, *Understanding racist activism*, 63–71.
44 Hochschild, *Strangers in their own land*, 15.
45 Worrying about one's nation as a form of 'affective investment in the nation', as Ghassan Hage has argued, is the predominant characteristic of a widespread contemporary wave of paranoid nationalism: see G. Hage, *Against paranoid nationalism. Searching for hope in a shrinking society* (Annandale, NSW: Pluto Press Australia, 2003), 3.
46 See Leser and Spissinger, 'The functionality of affects', 333.
47 Thanks to Steven Schäller for this observation.
48 See Leser and Spissinger, 'The functionality of affects', 333–334.
49 See Leser and Spissinger, 'The functionality of affects', 333.

Notes

50 The events described here are discussed in further detail in Leser and Spissinger, 'The functionality of affects', 333–334.
51 Ibid.
52 Ibid.
53 M. Herzfeld, 'How populism works', in D. Theodossopoulos and B. Kapferer (eds), *Democracy's paradox. Populism and its contemporary crisis* (New York: Berghahn, 2019), 135.
54 Hochschild, *Strangers in their own land*, 136–139.
55 Leser and Spissinger, 'The functionality of affects', 337.
56 T. Hestermann and E. Hoven, 'Kriminalität in Deutschland im Spiegel von Pressemitteilungen der Alternative für Deutschland (AfD)', *Kriminalpolitische Zeitschrift* 3 (2019), 127–139.
57 See Refcrime, *Refugee and Migrant Crime Map* (2019), URL: www. refcrime.info/en/Home/Index [Accessed 16 November 2019].
58 See ARD, *Kontraste. Pegida nach dem Mord an Walter Lübcke* [Video File] (7 July 2019), URL: www.youtube.com/ watch?v=rTvNqMSniAU [Accessed 17 May 2020].
59 Wodak, 'Entering the "post-shame era"'.
60 Leser and Spissinger, 'The functionality of affects', 338.
61 Ibid.
62 Thanks to Anna Bentzien for sharing with the authors her notes on this meeting.
63 Anna Bentzien points out that rumour has it that a truck loaded with bikes of the make Wolf overturned a few decades ago, and so the saga began. Email communication on 13 November 2019.
64 Ayata, 'Deutschland liegt in Sachsen', 263.

Notes to Chapter 6: Sheep in wolves' clothing?

1 Shoshan, *The management of hate*, 176.
2 Ibid., 142.
3 Fulbrook, 'The threat of the radical right in Germany'.
4 A. Reckwitz, *Die Gesellschaft der Singularitäten. Zum Strukturwandel der Moderne* (Berlin: Suhrkamp, 2017).
5 P. Manow, *(Ent-)Demokratisierung der Demokratie* (Berlin: Suhrkamp, 2020).
6 There is a new twitter thread on 'baseball bat years' referring to the 1990s, where victims recount their terrifying experiences with violent neo-Nazis – and the culture of impunity fostered by the local authorities.
7 The renowned political scientist Hajo Funke sees a right-wing insurrection in the making. After the Chemnitz riots, he said in an interview with the *Süddeutsche Zeitung*: 'We are observing an

established violent neo-nazi milieu [in Saxony ...] it has spread, amoeba-like, into everyday structures, into certain districts. It has established its own dog-wistling codes, it own communication networks. That is central. And nobody stopped them during the Chemnitz riots, not really. From this point on, from the 26th and 27th of August 2018, they have been telling themselves: This is our chance. In my mind, this was the initial spark for a nationalist revolution.' See S. Braun, 'Teile der rechtsradikalen Minderheit sind zu allem fähig', *Süddeutsche* (2 October 2018), URL: www. sueddeutsche.de/politik/rechtsextremismus-teile-der-rechtsradi kalen-minderheit-sind-zu-allem-faehig-1.4153961 [Accessed 17 May 2020].

8 Interview given to the authors on 9 November 2018 by Franz Kerker, AfD MP for the Berlin regional parliament, for the BBC programme *The Wolves Are Coming Back*.

References

Printed sources

Ahmed, S. (2014 [2004]). *The cultural politics of emotion*. Second edition. Edinburgh: Edinburgh University Press.

Akkerman, T. (2015). 'Gender and the radical right in Western Europe. A comparative analysis of policy agendas', *Patterns of Prejudice* 49(1–2), 37–60.

Appadurai, A. (2017). 'Democracy fatigue', in H. Geiselberger (ed.), *The Great Regression*. Cambridge; Malden: Polity Press.

Arzheimer, K. & C. C. Berning (2019). 'How the Alternative for Germany (AfD) and their voters veered to the radical right, 2013–2017', *Electoral Studies* 60, 102–140.

Aust, S. & D. Laabs (2014). *Heimatschutz. Der Staat und die Mordserie des NSU*. München: Pantheon.

Ayata, İ. (2017). 'Deutschland liegt in Sachsen', in H. Kleffner, M. Meisner, C. Ditsch & K. Stuttmann (eds), *Unter Sachsen. Zwischen Wut und Willkommen*. Berlin: Ch. Links Verlag, 260–264.

Babka von Gostomski, C., B. Küpper & W. Heitmeyer (2007). 'Fremdenfeindlichkeit in den Bundesländern. Die schwierige Lage in Ostdeutschland', in W. Heitmeyer (ed.), *Edition Suhrkamp: Vol. 2484. Deutsche Zustände, Folge 5*, Frankfurt am Main: Suhrkamp, 102–128.

Begrich, D. (2015). '"Wir sind das Pack". Von Hoyerswerda nach Heidenau', *Blätter für deutsche und internationale Politik* 60(10), 9–12.

Berger, P. A. & A. Weiß (2008). *Transnationalisierung sozialer Ungleichheit*. Wiesbaden: Springer VS. doi: 10.1007/978-3-531-91160-1.

References

Berking, H. (2006). 'Experiencing reunification. An East German village after the fall of the Wall', in L. Rudolph & J. K. Jacobsen (eds), *Experiencing the State*. Oxford: Oxford University Press, 143–164.

Berlant, L. (2011). *Cruel optimism*. Durham, NC: Duke University Press.

Best, H. (2017). 'Die Ausgangslage 1989/90. Elitenwechsel oder Elitenreproduktion?', in Deutsche Gesellschaft e.V. (ed.), *Ostdeutsche Eliten. Träume, Wirklichkeiten und Perspektiven*. Online Publikation: Deutsche Gesellschaften e.V., 36–45.

Billig, M. (1995). *Banal nationalism*. London: Sage.

Blee, K. M. (2003). 'Becoming a racist. Women in contemporary Ku Klux Klan and neo-Nazi groups', *Gender & Society* 10, 680–702.

Blee, K. M. (2003). *Inside organized racism. Women in the hate movement*. Berkeley, CA; London: University of California Press.

Blee, K. M. (2009). *Women of the Klan. Racism and gender in the 1920s*. Berkeley, CA; London: University of California Press.

Blee, K. M. (ed.) (2012). *Women of the right. Comparisons and interplay across borders*. University Park, PA: Pennsylvania State University Press.

Blee, K. M. (2018). *Understanding racist activism. Theory, methods and research*. London; New York: Routledge, Taylor & Francis Group.

Brauer, K. (2015). 'Bowling mit Wölfen. Rurale Gemeinden zwischen demographischem Untergang und (sozial-)kapitaler Zukunft', in U. Fachinger & H. Künemund (eds), *Gerontologie und ländlicher Raum. Lebensbedingungen, Veränderungsprozesse und Gestaltungsmöglichkeiten*, Wiesbaden: Springer VS, 45–74.

Braun, C. von (2017). 'anti-Genderismus. Über das Feindbild Geschlechterforschung', *Kursbuch* 192, 28–45.

Brennan, T. (2004). *The transmission of affect*. Ithaca: Cornell University Press.

Bromley, R. (2018). 'The politics of displacement. The Far Right narrative of Europe and its "others"', *From the European South* 3 (2018), 13–26.

Bruner, J. (1991). 'The narrative construction of reality', *Critical Inquiry* 18, 1–21.

Bundestag (1991). *Bundestag Document 11/8472*. Berlin: Bundestag.

Bundestag (2019). *Drucksache 19/7541*. Berlin: Bundestag.

Busher, J., P. Giurlando & G. B. Sullivan (2018). 'Introduction. The emotional dynamics of backlash politics beyond anger, hate, fear, pride, and loss', *Humanity & Society* 42(4), 399–409.

Butter, M. (2018). *Nichts ist, wie es scheint. Über Verschwörungstheorien*. Berlin: Suhrkamp.

References

Caramani, D. & L. Manucci (2019). 'National past and populism. The re-elaboration of fascism and its impact on right-wing populism in Western Europe', *West European Politics* 42(6), 1159–1187.

Cox, M. & M. Durham (2000). 'The politics of anger. The extreme right in the United States', in P. Hainsworth (ed.), *Politics of the extreme right. From the margins to the mainstream.* London: Bloomsbury, 287–311.

Cramer, K. J. (2016). *The politics of resentment. Rural consciousness in Wisconsin and the rise of Scott Walker.* Chicago; London: University of Chicago Press.

Czollek, M. (2018). *Desintegriert euch!* München: Carl Hanser Verlag.

Datt, T. (2017). 'Flucht aus Colditz. Eine rechtsfreie Zone im mittelsächsischen Hügelland', in H. Kleffner, M. Meisner, C. Ditsch & K. Stuttmann (eds), *Unter Sachsen. Zwischen Wut und Willkommen.* Berlin: Ch. Links Verlag, 211–225.

Davey, J. & J. Ebner (2019). '*The Great Replacement'. The violent consequences of mainstreamed extremism.* London: Institute for Strategic Dialogue.

Decker, F. (2008). 'Germany. Right-wing populist failures and left-wing successes', in D. Albertazzi and D. McDonnell (eds), *Twenty-first century populism. The spectre of Western European democracy.* Basingstoke: Palgrave, 119–134.

Decker, F. (2016). 'The "Alternative for Germany". Factors behind its emergence and profile of a new right-wing populist party', *German Politics and Society* 34(2), 1–16.

Dellenbaugh-Losse, M., J. Homeyer, J. Leser & R. Pates (2020). 'Toxische Orte? Faktoren der regionalen Anfälligkeit für völkischen Nationalismus', in L. Berg & J. Üblacker (eds), *Rechtes Denken – Rechte Räume.* Bielefeld: transcript, pp. 47–82.

Dieschereit, E. (2014). *Blumen für Otello. Über die Verbrechen von Jena.* Berlin: Secession Verlag.

Donovan, J. (2012). *The Way of Men.* Milwaukee: Dissonant Hum. [E-book edition].

Ebner, J. (2017). *The rage. The vicious circle of Islamist and far-right extremism.* London: I. B. Tauris & Co. Ltd.

Ellerbrock, D., L. Koch, S. Müller-Mall, M. Münkler, J. Scharloth, D. Schrage & G. Schwerhoff (2017). 'Invektivität – Perspektiven eines neuen Forschungsprogramms in den Kultur- und Sozialwissenschaften', *Kulturwissenschaftliche Zeitschrift* 2(1), 2–24.

El-Tayeb, F. (2016). *Undeutsch. Die Konstruktion des Anderen in der postmigrantischen Gesellschaft.* Bielefeld: transcript Verlag.

Emcke, C. (2019). *Against hate.* Cambridge: Polity Press.

References

Engler, W. (1992). *Die zivilisatorische Lücke. Versuche über den Staatssozialismus.* Frankfurt am Main: Suhrkamp.

Engler, W. (1995). *Die ungewollte Moderne. Ost-West-Passagen.* Frankfurt am Main: Suhrkamp.

Erdem, I. (2006). 'Anti-deutsche Linke oder anti-linke Deutsche? Eine sachliche Betrachtung', *UTOPIE kreativ* 192 (Oktober 2006), 926–939.

Erices, R. (2018). 'Hetzjagd im Augst 1975 in Erfurt. Wie Ausländerfeindlichkeit in der DDR verharmlost und verleugnet wurde', *Gerbergasse 18. Thüringer Vierteljahreszeitschrift für Zeitgeschichte und Politik* 89(4), 22–25.

Ewing, P. & S. Silbey (1995). 'Subversive stories and hegemonic tales. Toward a sociology of narrative', *Law and Society Review* 29, 197–226.

Fachinger, U. & H. Künemund (eds) (2015). *Gerontologie und ländlicher Raum. Lebensbedingungen, Veränderungsprozesse und Gestaltungsmöglichkeiten.* Wiesbaden: Springer VS.

Federal Government Commissioner for the New Federal States (2018). *Annual Report of the Federal Government on the Status of German Unity 2018.* Berlin: Federal Ministry for Economic Affairs and Energy.

Feola, M. (2015). 'Fear and loathing in democratic times', *Political Studies* 64, 53–69.

Flack, A. (2018). 'Continental creatures. Animals in contemporary European history', *Contemporary European History* 27(3), 517–529, doi: 10.1017/S0960777318000036.

Forchtner, B. (2019). 'Nation, nature, purity. Extreme-right biodiversity in Germany', *Patterns of Prejudice* 53:3, 285–301, doi: 10.1080/0031322X.2019.1592303.

Forchtner B. and Ö. Özvatan (2019). 'Beyond the "German Forest". Environmental communication by the far right in Germany,' in B. Forchtner (ed.), *The far right and the environment.* Abingdon; New York: Routledge.

Foroutan, N., F. Kalter, C. Canan & M. Simon (2019). *Ost-Migrantische Analogien I. Konkurrenz um Anerkennung.* Unter Mitarbeit von Daniel Kubiak und Sabrina Zajak. Berlin: DeZIM-Institut.

Franke, N. (2013). 'Rechtsextremismus und Ökolandbau. Ganzheitlich und organisch mit braunem Anstrich', *Ökologie und Landbau* 165, 2013(1), 50–52.

Fuchs, C., & P. Middelhoff (2019). *Das Netzwerk der neuen Rechten. Wer sie lenkt, wer sie finanziert und wie sie die Gesellschaft verändern.* Reinbek bei Hamburg: Rowohlt.

Fulbrook, M. (1994). 'The threat of the radical right in Germany', *Patterns of Prejudice* 28(3–4), 57–66.

References

Garland, J. & J. Treadwell (2012). 'The new politics of hate? An assessment of the appeal of the English Defence League amongst disadvantaged white working-class communities in England', *Journal of Hate Studies* 10(1), 123–142.

Geipel, I. (2019). *Umkämpfte Zone. Mein Bruder, der Osten und der Hass.* Stuttgart: Klett-Cotta.

Gest, J. (2016). *The new minority.* New York: Oxford University Press.

Goebbels, J. (1935). 'Was wollen wir im Reichstag?', in H. S. van Berk (ed.), *Der Angriff, Aufsätze aus der Kampfzeit.* München: Franz Eher Nachfolger [Reprint].

Grabow, K. (2016). 'PEGIDA and the Alternative für Deutschland. Two sides of the same coin?', *European View* 15(2): 173–181.

Habermas, J. (1998). *Faktizität und Geltung. Beiträge zur Diskurstheorie des Rechts und des demokratischen Rechtsstaats.* Frankfurt am Main: Suhrkamp.

Hacking, I. (1999). *The social construction of what?* Cambridge, MA: Harvard University Press.

Hage, G. (2003). *Against paranoid nationalism. Searching for hope in a shrinking society.* Annandale, NSW: Pluto Press Australia.

Hambauer, V. & A. Mays (2017). 'Wer wählt die AfD?', *Zeitschrift für Vergleichende Politikwissenschaft* 1(2018), 133–154.

Hansen, M. A., & J. Olsen (2019). 'Flesh of the same flesh. A study of voters for the Alternative for Germany (AfD) in the 2017 federal election', *German Politics* 28(1), 1–19.

Harding, S., & K. Stewart (2003). 'Anxieties of influence: Conspiracy theory and therapeutic culture in millenial America', in H. G. West & T. Sanders (eds), *Transparency and conspiracy: Ethnographies of suspicion in the new world order.* Durham, NC: Duke University Press, 258–286.

Harteveld, E., W. Van Der Brug, S. Dahlberg & A. Kokkonen (2015). 'The gender gap in populist radical-right voting. Examining the demand side in Western and Eastern Europe', *Patterns of Prejudice* 49(1–2), 103–134.

Hartleb, F. (2018). *Einsame Wölfe. Der neue Terrorismus rechter Einzeltäter.* Hamburg: Hoffmann und Campe.

Hartshorn Dellenbaugh, M. (2013). *Landscape changes in East Berlin after 1989. A comprehensive grounded theory analysis through three case studies.* Dissertation. Berlin: Humboldt-Universität zu Berlin.

Henderson, V. L. (2008). 'Is there hope for anger? The politics of spatializing and (re)producing an emotion', *Emotion, Space and Society* 1(1) 28–37.

References

Herzfeld, M. (2019). 'How populism works', in D. Theodossopoulos & B. Kapferer (eds), *Democracy's paradox. Populism and its contemporary crisis*. New York: Berghahn, 122–138.

Hestermann, T. & E. Hoven (2019). 'Kriminalität in Deutschland im Spiegel von Pressemitteilungen der Alternative für Deutschland (AfD)', *Kriminalpolitische Zeitschrift* 3/2019, 127–139.

Hochschild, A. R. (2016). *Strangers in their own land. Anger and mourning on the American right.* New York; London: The New Press.

Höcke, B. & S. Hennig (2018). *Nie zweimal in denselben Fluss.* Lüdinghausen: Manuscriptum.

Inglehart, R. F. & P. Norris (2016). *Trump, Brexit, and the Rise of Populism. Economic Have-nots and Cultural Backlash,* Harvard Kennedy School. Faculty Research Working Paper. Series RWP 16-026, August.

Intelmann, D. (2019). Sieben Thesen zur urbanen Krise von Chemnitz. *sub/urban. Zeitschrift für kritische Stadtforschung* 7(1/2), 189–202.

IWH – Leibniz-Institut für Wirtschaftsforschung Halle (eds) (2019). *Vereintes Land – drei Jahrzehnte nach dem Mauerfall.* Halle: Leibniz-Institut für Wirtschaftsforschung.

Jennerjahn, M. (2016). 'Programme und Projekte gegen Rechtsextremismus vor Ort – Das Fallbeispiel Sachsen', in S. Braun, A. Geisler & M. Gerster (eds), *Strategien der extremen Rechten. Hintergründe, Analysen, Antworten.* Second edition. Wiesbaden: Springer VS.

Kleffner, H., & A. Spangenberg (eds) (2016). *Generation Hoyerswerda. Das Netzwerk militanter Neonazis in Brandenburg.* Berlin-Brandenburg: Be.bra Verlag.

Kleine-Hartlage, M. (2017). 'Der entfesselte Westen. Islam und der Tumor des Liberalismus', in *Compact – Magazin für Souveränität* 2017(5), 38–39.

Kollmorgen, R. (2017). 'Ostdeutsche in den Eliten. Problemdimensionen und Zukunftsperspektiven.', in Deutsche Gesellschaft e.V. (ed.), *Ostdeutsche Eliten. Träume, Wirklichkeiten und Perspektiven.* Online Publikation: Deutsche Gesellschaften e.V., 54–65.

Kølvraa, C. (2020). 'Wolves in sheep's clothing? The Danish far right and "wild nature"', in B. Forchtner (ed.), *The far right and the environment. Politics, discourse and communication.* London and New York: Routledge.

Koppetsch, C. (2019). *Die Gesellschaft des Zorns. Rechtspopulismus im globalen Zeitalter.* Bielefeld: transcript.

Köpping, P. (2018). *Integriert doch erst mal uns! Eine Streitschrift für den Osten.* Berlin: Ch. Links.

References

Köttig, M., R. Bitzan & A. Petö (eds) (2017). *Gender and far right politics in Europe.* Cham: Palgrave Macmillan.

Kowalczuk, I.-S. (2019). *Die Übernahme. Wie Ostdeutschland Teil der Bundesrepublik wurde.* München: C. H. Beck.

Kubitschek, G. (2019). 'Sachsen', in *Sezession. Sachsen* 90 (June), 1.

Lange, S. L. de & L. M. Mügge (2015). 'Gender and right-wing populism in the Low Countries. Ideological variations across parties and time', *Patterns of Prejudice* 49(1–2), 61–80.

Leser, J. & F. Spissinger (2020). 'The functionality of affects. Conceptualizing far-right populist politics beyond negative emotions', *Global Discourse* 10(2), 325–342.

Leser, J., F. Spissinger, J. Homeyer & T. Neidel (2020). 'Performing "resistance" – the far right's master narrative', *The Journal of Culture* 8(1), 13–21.

Levitsky, J. & D. Ziblatt (2018). *How democracies die.* New York: Broadway Books.

Manow, P. (2020). *(Ent-) Demokratisierung der Demokratie.* Berlin: edition Suhrkamp.

Mau, S. (2007). *Transnationale Vergesellschaftung. Die Entgrenzung sozialer Lebenswelten.* Frankfurt am Main; New York: Campus.

Mau, S. (2019). *Lütten Klein. Leben in der ostdeutschen Transformationsgesellschaft.* Berlin: Suhrkamp.

Megre, W. (2003). *Anastasia. Tochter der Taiga*, trans. H. Kunkel. Zürich: Govinda Verlag.

Meiering, D., A. Dziri, N. Foroutan, S. Teune, E. Lehnert & M. Abou Taam (2018). *Brückennarrative. Verbindende Elemente in der Radikalisierung von Gruppen.* Frankfurt am Main: Leibniz-Institut Hessische Stiftung Friedens- und Konfliktforschung (HSFK).

Miller-Idriss, C. (2018). 'The United German extreme right', *Centre for Analysis of the Radical Right*, URL: www.radicalrightanalysis. com/2018/09/10/the-united-german-extreme-right/ [Accessed 25 June 2019].

Minkenberg, M. (1998). *Die neue radikale Rechte im Vergleich. USA, Frankreich, Deutschland.* Opladen: Westdeutscher Verlag.

Minkenberg, M. (2017). *The radical right in Eastern Europe. Democracy under siege?* New York: Palgrave Macmillan.

Mishra, P. (2017). *Age of anger. A history of the present.* London: Allen Lane.

Most, E. (2009). *Fünfzig Jahre im Auftrag des Kapitals.* Berlin: Das Neue Berlin.

Mouffe, C. (2018). *For a left populism.* London; New York: Verso.

Mounk, Y. (2018). *The people vs. democracy.* Cambridge, MA: Harvard University Press.

References

Mudde, C. (2016). *On extremism and democracy in Europe*. London New York: Routledge.

Mudde, C. (2019). *The far right today*. Cambridge; Medford: Polity Press.

Müller-Mertens, M. (2017). '"Dass ein gutes Deutschland blühe". Das patriotische Erbe der SED', *Compact – Magazin für Souveränität* 2017(5), 20–21.

Müller-Mertens, M. (2017). 'Deutsche demokratische Reserve. Bürgerprotest zwischen Elbe und Oder', *Compact – Magazin für Souveränität* 2017(5), 14–16.

Ngai, S. (2007). *Ugly feelings*. Cambridge, MA: Harvard University Press.

Niedermayer, O., & J. Hofrichter (2016). 'Die Wählerschaft der AfD. Wer ist sie, woher kommt sie und wie weit rechts steht sie?', *ZParl Zeitschrift für Parlamentsfragen* 47(2), 267–285.

Olsen, J. (2000). 'The perils of rootedness. On bioregionalism and right wing ecology in Germany', *Landscape Journal* 19(1–2), 73–83.

Ogman, R. (2013). *Against the nation – Anti-national politics in Germany*. Porsgrunn: New Compass Press.

Özvatan, Ö. & B. Forchtner (2019). 'The far-right Alternative für Deutschland in Germany. Towards a "happy ending"?', in A. Waring (ed.), *The new authoritarianism. Vol. 2: A risk analysis of the European alt-right phenomenon*. Stuttgart: ibidem, 199–226.

Panayi, P. (1994). 'Racial violence in the new Germany 1990–93', *Contemporary European History* 3(3), 265–287.

Pates, R. (2011). 'Die Hölle sind immer die anderen. Moralische Ordnungen in Trainings gegen "Rechtsextremisten"', in FKR (ed.), *Ordnung. Macht. Extremismus. Effekte und Alternativen des Extremismusmodells*. Wiesbaden: VS Verlag für Sozialwissenschaften, 212–239.

Pates, R. & M. Schochow (eds) (2013). *Der 'Ossi'. Mikropolitische Studien über einen symbolischen Ausländer*. Wiesbaden: Springer VS.

Patton, D. F. (2017). 'Monday, Monday. Eastern protest movements and German party politics since 1989', *German Politics* 26(4), 480–497.

Patzelt, W. J. (2018). 'Mängel in der Responsivität oder Störungen in der Kommunikation? Deutschlands Repräsentationslücke und die AfD', *ZParl Zeitschrift für Parlamentsfragen* 49(4), 885–895.

Pickel, G. (2016). 'Eine sächsische politische Kultur des Extremismus?', in G. Pickel & O. Decker (eds), *Extremismus in Sachsen. Eine kritische Bestandsaufnahme*. Leipzig: Edition Leipzig, 16–26.

References

Pilkington, H. (2016). *Loud and proud. Passion and politics in the English Defence League.* Manchester: Manchester University Press.

Pollack, D. (1990). 'Das Ende einer Organisationsgesellschaft. Systemtheoretische Überlegungen zum gesellschaftlichen Umbruch in der DDR', *Zeitschrift für Soziologie* 19(4), 292–307.

Pötzl, N. (2019). *Der Treuhand-Komplex. Legenden. Fakten. Emotionen.* Hamburg: kursbuch.edition.

Powell, C. (1992). 'What the PM learnt about the Germans', in H. James & M. Stone (eds), *When the Wall came down. Reactions to German unification.* New York; London: Routledge, 233–239.

Präkels, M. (2017). *Als ich mit Hitler Schnapskirsche aß.* Berlin: Verbrecher Verlag.

Przybyszewski, A. (2019). 'Ex Oriente Lux', *Sezession* 90, June.

Quent, M. (2019). *Deutschland rechts außen. Wie die Rechten nach der Macht greifen und wie wir sie stoppen können.* München: Piper.

Rawls, J. (1996). *Political liberalism,* New York: Columbia University Press.

Reckwitz, A. (2017). *Die Gesellschaft der Singularitäten. Zum Strukturwandel der Moderne.* Berlin: Suhrkamp.

Retterath, J. (2008). 'Volk', in I. Haar, M. Fahlbusch & M. Berg (eds), *Handbuch der völkischen Wissenschaften.* München: Personen – Institutionen – Forschungsprogramme – Stiftungen.

Richter, F. (2018). *Hört endlich zu! Weil Demokratie Auseinandersetzung braucht.* Berlin: Ullstein.

Rietzschel, L. (2018). *Mit der Faust in die Welt schlagen.* Berlin: Ullstein Verlag.

Röpke, A. & A. Speit (2019). *Völkische Landnahme. Alte Sippen, junge Siedler, rechte Ökos.* Berlin: Links.

Rösel, F. (2019). 'Die Wucht der deutschen Teilung wird völlig unterschätzt', *Ifo Dresden berichtet* 3/2019, 23–25.

Rosellini, J. J. (2019). *The German new right. AfD, PEGIDA, and the re-imagining of German identity.* London: Hurst Publishers.

Sauer, B. (2018). 'Demokratie, Volk und Geschlecht. Radikaler Rechtspopulismus in Europa', in K., Pühl & B. Sauer (eds), *Kapitalismuskritische Gesellschaftsanalyse. Queer-feministische Positionen.* Münster: Westfälisches Dampfboot, 178–195.

Sax, B. (2000). *Animals in the Third Reich. Pets, scapegoats and the Holocaust.* New York: Continuum.

Schildt, A. (2004). '"German Angst": Überlegungen zur Mentalitätsgeschichte der Bundesrepublik', in D. Münkel & J. Schwarzkopf (eds), *Geschichte als Experiment. Studien zu Politik, Kultur und Alltag im 19. und 20. Jahrhundert.* Frankfurt am Main: Campus Verlag, 87–97.

References

Schmidt, A. (n.d.). *Völkische Siedler/innen im ländlichen Raum.* Berlin: Amadeu Antonio Stiftung.

Schmidt, D., R. Pates & S. Karawanskij (2011). 'Verwaltung politischer Devianz'. Das Problem des Wissens', in FKR (ed.), *Ordnung. Macht. Extremismus. Effekte und Alternativen des Extremismusmodells,* Wiesbaden: VS Verlag für Sozialwissenschaften, 191–211.

Schwarzbözl, T. & M. Fatke (2016). 'Außer Protesten nichts gewesen? Das politische Potenzial der AfD', in *Politische Vierteljahresschrift* 57(2), 276–299. doi: 10.5771/0032-3470-2016-2-276.

Schwörer, J. (2019). 'Alternative für Deutschland: from the streets to the Parliament?', in M. Caiani and O. Císař (eds), *Radical right movement parties in Europe,* New York: Routledge, 29–45.

Seidel, J. (2019). 'Warum Sachsen? Warum der Osten?', *Sezession. Sachsen,* 90 (June).

Shoshan, N. (2016). *The management of hate. Nation, affect and the governance of right-wing extremism in Germany.* Princeton: Princeton University Press.

Somers, M. (1994). 'The narrative constitution of identity. A relational and network approach', *Theory and Society* 23, 605–649.

Spierings, N. & A. Zaslove (2015). 'Gendering the vote for populist radical-right parties', *Patterns of Prejudice* 49(1–2), 135–162.

Valluvan, S. (2017). 'Defining and challenging the new nationalism', *Juncture* 23(4), 232–239.

Virilio, P. (2012). *The administration of fear.* Los Angeles: Semiotext(e).

Weiß, V. (2017). *Die autoritäre Revolte. Die Neue Rechte und der Untergang des Abendlandes.* Stuttgart: Klett-Cotta.

Wiegel, G. (2016). 'Rechte Erlebniswelten', in M. Dust, I. Lohmann & G. Steffens (eds), *Events and edutainment. Jahrbuch für Pädagogik 2016.* Frankfurt am Main: Peter Lang, 95–106.

Winkler, G. (1994). *Sozialreport 1994. Daten und Fakten zur sozialen Lage in den neuen Bundesländern.* Berlin: GSFP.

Wodak, R. (2015). *The politics of fear. What right-wing populist discourses mean.* London: Sage.

Wodak, R. (2019). 'Entering the "post-shame era". The rise of illiberal democracy, populism and neo-authoritarianism in Europe', *Global Discourse* 9(1), 195–213.

Woods, R. (2007). *Germany's New Right as Culture and Politics.* Basingstoke and New York: Palgrave Macmillan.

Wowtscherk, C. (2014). *Was wird, wenn die Zeitbombe hochgeht? Eine sozialgeschichtliche Analyse der fremdenfeindlichen Ausschreitungen in Hoyerswerda im September 1991.* Göttingen: V & R Unipress.

References

Zuckerberg, D. (2018). *Not all dead white men. Classics and misogyny in the digital age.* Cambridge, MA: Harvard University Press.

Internet sources

Antifa in Leipzig (14 October 2014). 'Colditz: Neonazi mit Crystal Meth aufgegriffen', *Inventati*. URL: www.inventati.org/leipzig/?p=2513 [Accessed 2 November 2019].

ARD (7 July 2019). *Kontraste: Pegida nach dem Mord an Walter Lübcke* [Video file]. URL: www.youtube.com/watch?v=rTvNqMSniAU [Accessed 17 May 2020].

Bender, J. & R. Bingener (15 January 2016). 'Marc Jongen: Parteiphilosoph der AfD', *FAZ*. URL: www.faz.net/aktuell/poli tik/inland/marc-jongen-ist-afd-politiker-und-philosoph-14005731. html [Accessed 16 November 2020].

Bpb – Bundeszentrale für politische Bildung (Federal Agency for Civic Education) (2015). *Das Vermögen der DDR und die Privatisierung durch die Treuhand.* URL: www.bpb.de/geschichte/deutsche-ein heit/zahlen-und-fakten-zur-deutschen-einheit/211280/das-vermo egen-der-ddr-und-die-privatisierung-durch-die-treuhand [Accessed 17 May 2020].

Bundesamt für Justiz (28 March 2019). *Basic Law for the Federal Republic of Germany.* URL: www.gesetze-im-internet.de/eng lisch_gg/englisch_gg.html#po111 [Accessed 3 November 2019].

Braun, S. (2 October 2018). 'Teile der rechtsradikalen Minderheit sind zu allem fähig', *Süddeutsche*. URL: www.sueddeutsche.de/politik/ rechtsextremismus-teile-der-rechtsradikalen-minderheit-sind-zu-allem-faehig-1.4153961 [Accessed 17 May 2020].

Brecht, B. (1950). 'Children's Hymn', *Wikipedia*. URL: https:// en.wikipedia.org/wiki/Children%27s_Hymn [Accessed 17 May 2020].

Bülow, B. von (11 December 1899). *Bülow's 'Hammer and Anvil' Speech before the Reichstag.* URL: wwi.lib.byu.edu/index.php/ Bülow%27s_%27Hammer_and_Anvil%27_Speech_before_the_ Reichstag [Accessed 3 November 2019].

Cagle, S. (16 August 2019). '"Bees, not refugees": The environmentalist roots of anti-immigrant bigotry', *The Guardian*. URL: www. theguardian.com/environment/2019/aug/15/anti [Accessed 4 November 2019].

Carstens, P. (19 November 2018). 'Raben für mehr tote Schafe verantwortlich als Wölfe', *GEO*. URL: www.geo.de/natur/tierwelt/ 19945-rtkl-tausende-tote-laemmer-raben-fuer-mehr-tote-schafe-verantwortlich-als [Accessed 17 May 2020].

References

DBBW (2019). *Dokumentations- und Beratungsstelle des Bundes zum Thema Wolf*. URL: www.dbb-wolf.de/ [Accessed 16 November 2019].

Decker, M. (31 October 2017). 'Bpb-Chef über westdeutsche Dominanz: Es fehlen Übersetzer.' *Berliner Zeitung*. URL: www.berliner-zeitung.de/politik/bpb-chef-ueber-westdeutsche-dominanz--es-fehlen-uebersetzer-kultureller-differenzen--28746484 [Accessed 25 October 2019].

Der Flügel (11 July 2018). *Kyffhäusertreffen 2018 – Rede von Björn Höcke* [Video file]. URL: www.youtube.com/watch?v=kbLikMxEsqk [Accessed 17 May 2020].

Deter, A. (6 March 2018). 'Schäfer in Not: Zahl der Berufsschäfer jetzt unter 1000!', *topagrar online*. URL: www.topagrar.com/management-und-politik/news/schaefer-in-not-zahl-der-berufsschaefer-jetzt-unter-1000-9410439.html [Accessed 17 May 2020].

Deutscher Jagdverband (29 May 2018). 'Achtung Falschmeldung!' URL: www.jagdverband.de/content/achtung-falschmeldung [Accessed 16 November 2019].

Ecke, M. (2018). 'What Does Chemnitz Tell Us About The Growth Of Right-Wing Radicalism In Germany?', *Social Europe*, URL: www.socialeurope.eu/what-does-chemnitz-tell-us-about-the-growth-of-right-wing-radicalism-in-germany [Accessed 25 June 2019].

Focus Online (6 June 2018). *Strafanzeige gegen Gauland wegen Verdachts auf Volksverhetzung*. URL: www.focus.de/politik/deutschland/vogelschiss-aeusserung-strafanzeige-gegen-gauland-wegen-verdachts-auf-volksverhetzung_id_9049620.html [Accessed 4 November 2019].

Förderverein der Deutschen Schafhaltung (29 April 2020). 'Deutsche Schäfer sind fassungslos und wütend: "Warum lässt uns die Gesellschaft im Stich?"', *Wir Lieben Schafe: Pressemitteilungen*. URL: www.wir-lieben-schafe.com/pressemitteilungen/ [Accessed 17 May 2020].

Frohnmaier, M. (26 August 2018). 'Wenn der Staat die Bürger nicht mehr schützen kann, gehen die Menschen auf die Straße und schützen sich selber. Ganz einfach! Heute ist es Bürgerpflicht, die todbringendendie "Messermigration" zu stoppen! Es hätte deinen Vater, Sohn oder Bruder treffen können!', *Twitter*. URL: www.twitter.com/Frohnmaier_AfD/status/1033806135990644744 [Accessed 3 November 2019].

Funke, H. (3 October 2018). 'Eine Minderheit, die zu allem fähig ist', *Süddeutsche Zeitung*. URL: www.sueddeutsche.de/politik/chemnitz-eine-minderheit-die-zu-allem-faehig-ist-1.4154943 [Accessed 16 November 2019].

References

Gebhardt, R. (2018). 'Hauptfeind Liberalismus', *Magazin 'der rechte rand' Ausgabe 173 – Juli/August 2018*. URL: www.der-rechte-rand. de/archive/3461/thor-von-waldstein-liberalismus/ [Accessed 3 November 2019].

Gruntert, J. (28 August 2018). 'Der Abend, an dem der Rechtsstaat aufgab', *Zeit Online*. URL: www.zeit.de/gesellschaft/zeitgesche hen/2018-08/chemnitz-rechte-demonstration-ausschreitungen-polizei [Accessed 3 November 2019].

Haselrieder, M. and J. Bartz (20 August 2019). 'Mit der Angst auf Stimmenfang: Der Wolf im Wahlkampf der AfD in Sachsen', *ZDF*. URL: www.zdf.de/nachrichten/heute/mit-der-angst-auf-stimmen fang-der-wolf-im-wahlkampf-der-afd-100.html.

Hennings, A. (17 March 2019). 'Kampf um die Matten – Wie die rechte Szene den Kampfsport instrumentalisiert', *Deutschlandfunk*. URL: www.deutschlandfunkkultur.de/kampf-um-die-matten-wie-die-rechte-szene-den-kampfsport.966.de.html?dram:article_id=443785 [Accessed 4 November 2019].

Hilse, Karsten (21 February 2019). 'Wolfsmanagement und -moni-toring', *Deutscher Bundestag: Parlamentsfernsehen*. URL: www. bundestag.de/mediathek?videoid=7328919#url=L21lZGlhdGhla2 92ZXJsYXk/dmlkZW9pZDo3MzI4OTE5JnZpZGVvaWQ9NzMyMyO DkxOSZ2aWRlb2lkPTczMjg5MTk=&mod=mediathek [Accessed 24 November 2019].

Hilse, K. (24 October 2019). 'Bundesnaturschutzgesetz und Wolfsmanagement', *Deutscher Bundestag: Parlamentsfernsehen*. URL: www.bundestag.de/mediathek?videoid=7397423#url=L21lZ GlhdGhla292ZXJsYXk/dmlkZW9pZDo3Mzk3NDIzJnZpZGVvaW Q9NzM5NzQyMw==&mod=mediathek [Accessed 10 May 2020].

kanal schnellroda (13 March 2017). *Violence is Golden – Jack Donovan beim IfS* [Video file]. URL: www.youtube.com/ watch?v=4v48H9FreyY [Accessed 3 November 2019].

Knapstein, B. (22 May 2018). 'Erstmals Wolfsjagd auf Pferde beo-bachtet', *Böhme-Zeitung*. URL: western-journal.de/2018/05/22/ boehme-zeitung-18-mai-2018-erstmals-wolfsjagd-auf-pferde-beobachtet/[Accessed 16 November 2019].

Kuhn, D. (25 November 2012). 'Unsere andere Fahne', Politically Incorrect. URL: www.pi-news.net/2011/09/unsere-andere-fahne/ [Accessed 16 November 2019].

Kummetz, D., J. Schaar, N. Hotsch & J. Jacobsen (27 February 2020). 'Interaktive Karte: Wölfe in Schleswig-Holstein', *NDR 1 Welle Nord.*, URL: www.ndr.de/nachrichten/schleswig-holstein/ Interaktive-Karte-Woelfe-in-Schleswig-Holstein,wolf3736.html [Accessed 17 May 2020].

References

Laak, C. van (14 September 2019). 'Gefühlte Realität. AfD-Wahlkampf im Berlin', *Deutschlandfunk*. URL: www.deutschlandfunk.de/afd-wahlkampf-in-berlin-gefuehlte-realitaet.1773.de.html?dram:art icle_id=365806 [Accessed 2 October 2019].

Lanzke, A. (7 November 2012). 'Grüne Tarnfarbe: Rechtsextremismus unter dem Deckmantel des Umweltschutzes', *Belltower News*. URL: www.belltower.news/gruene-tarnfarbe-rechtsextremismus-unter-dem-deckmantel-des-umweltschutzes-35444/ [Accessed 4 November 2019].

Leber, S. (21 September 2017). 'Rechte vor Einzug in den Bundestag. So extrem sind die Kandidaten der AfD', *Tagesspiegel*. URL: www.tagesspiegel.de/themen/reportage/rechte-vor-einzug-in-den-bundestag-so-extrem-sind-die-kandidaten-der-afd/20350578.html [Accessed 4 November 2019].

Locke, S. (1 October 2018). '"Revolution Chemnitz": Eine selbsternannte Bürgerwehr', *FAZ*. URL: www.faz.net/aktuell/politik/in land/revolution-chemnitz-eine-selbsternannte-buergerwehr-15816 565.html [Accessed 25 October 2019].

Lohse, E. (3 August 2019). 'Westdeutsche AfD Politiker. Geliebter Anführer aus dem Lager des Feindes', *FAZ*. URL: www.faz.net/ aktuell/politik/inland/wieso-es-afd-wortfuehrern-nuetzt-wenn-sie-westdeutsche-sind-16315709.html [Accessed 3 November 2019];

Lübbe, S. (1 November 2019). 'Junge AfD-Wähler: Überzeugungswähler', *Zeit Campus*. URL: www.zeit.de/campus/2019-10/junge-afd-waeh ler-erfurt-thueringen-landtagswahl.

Maier, G. (5 October 2020). 'Thüringens Innenminister Maier zur rechten Unterwanderung: "Die Gleichgültigkeit ist das eigentliche Gift"', *Deutschlandfunk*. URL: www.deutschlandfunk. de/thueringens-innenminister-maier-zur-rechten-unterwander ung.694.de.html?dram:article_id=460373 [Accessed 14 November 2019].

Manthe, B. (2018). 'Scenes of "civil" war? Radical right narratives on Chemnitz', *Centre for Analysis of the Radical Right*. URL: www. radicalrightanalysis.com/2018/10/17/scenes-of-civil-war-radical-right-narratives-on-chemnitz/ [Accessed 25 June 2019].

Matthie, C. (17 January 2018). 'Wie sich Frauen vor Migranten-Gewalt schützen können', *Deutschland Kurier*. URL: www.deutschland-kurier.org/wie-sich-frauen-vor-migranten-gewalt-schuetzen-koen nen/ [Accessed 16 June 2019].

Megre, W. (2019). 'love productions', *Anastasia Website*. URL: www.loveproductions.org/deutsch/raum-der-liebe/ [Accessed 16 November 2019].

References

Meister, A., A. Biselli & M. Reuter (28 January 2019). 'Wir veröffentlichen das Verfassungsschutz-Gutachten zur AfD', *Netzpolitik.org.* URL: netzpolitik.org/2019/wir-veroeffentlichen-das-verfassungss chutz-gutachten-zur-afd/#2019–01–15_BfV-AfD-Gutachten_Que lle-265 [Accessed 14 November 2019].

Merkur (14 June 2019). *Ost-AfD im Steigflug – und viele Westdeutsche am Schalthebel.* URL: www.merkur.de/politik/ost-afd-im-steig flug-und-viele-westdeutsche-am-schalthebel-zr-12441394.html [Accessed 25 October 2019].

NABU (6 March 2018). 'Forsa-Umfrage zum Wolf: Zustimmung in der Bevölkerung bleibt hoch. Miller: Klima für die Akzeptanz des Wolfes ist nach wie vor gut', *Nabu Presseportal.* URL: www.presse portal.de/pm/6347/3928649 [Accessed 17 May 2020].

Refcrime (2019). *Refugee and Migrant Crime Map.* URL: www.ref crime.info/en/Home/Index [Accessed 16 November 2019].

Rosga, A. (2018). 'Anastasia-Bewegung – ein (un-)politisches Siedlungskonzept? Qualitative Feldforschung zu den Hintergründen und gesellschaftspolitischen Einstellungen innerhalb der Anastasia-Bewegung', in FARN. Retrieved from www.nf-farn.de/system/files/ documents/rosga_anastasia-bewegung.pdf [Accessed 3 November 2019].

Schulz, D. (1 October 2018). 'Wir waren wie Brüder. Jugendliche in Ostdeutschland', *FAZ.* URL: www.taz.de/Jugendliche-in-Ostdeutschland/!5536453/ [Accessed 3 November 2019].

Spiegel Online (29 August 2015). *Der Spiegel 36/2015 – Inhaltsverzeichnis.* www.spiegel.de/spiegel/print/index-2015-36. html [Accessed 4 November 2019].

Swan, B. (13 April 2017). 'Inside Virginia's Creep White-Power Wolf Cult', *Daily Beast.* URL: www.thedailybeast.com/inside-virginias-creepy-white-power-wolf-cult [Accessed 5 November 2019].

Tagesschau, *Halbjahresbilanz 2019: Bereits mehr als 8600 rechte Straftaten* (14 August 2020), URL: www.tagesschau.de/inland/krim inalitaet-rechtsextremismus-101.html?fbclid=IwAR22YH73Ree-rYTMZRGdNRspWYRS4hGSVLQGvGX3tdaKbHVBFRO61X gISSk [Accessed 17 May 2020].

Umwelt & Aktiv (n.d.). *Das Magazin für gesamtheitliches Denken: Umweltschutz, Tierschutz, Heimatschutz.* URL: www.umweltun daktiv.de [Accessed 5 November 2019].

Urahnenerbe Germania (n.d.). *Urahnenerbe Germania: Willkommen.* URL: www.urahnenerbe.de [Accessed 5 November 2019].

Vetter, A., A. Humburg & L. Mallien (2017). 'Anastasia – die Macht eines Phantoms', *OYA 45,* URL: http://oya-online.de/article/

References

read/2777-anastasia_die_macht_eines_phantoms.html?omit_overlay=59fa8b5371da6 [Accessed 5 November 2019].

Völkischer Aufklärer, 'Die Wölfe im Schafspelz oder die fast perfekte Täuschung', *Blogeintrag in Völkischer Aufklärer: Informationen für das deutsche Volk!* (16 February 2019), URL: www.voelkischer-aufklaerer.de/2019/02/16/die-woelfe-im-schafspelz-oder-die-fast-perfekte-taeuschung/) [Accessed 5 November 2019].

Wagenknecht, S. (30 November 2018). 'Wagenknecht lehnt offene Grenzen und Migrationspakt ab', URL: www.swr.de/swraktuell/Linken-Fraktionschefin-im-SWR-Interview-Wagenknecht-lehnt-offene-Grenzen-und-Migrationspakt-ab,interview-d-woche-wagenknecht-100.html [Accessed 16 November 2019].

wahlrecht.de (27 October 2019). 'Stimmenanteile der AfD bei den jeweils letzten Landtagswahlen in den Bundesländern bis Oktober 2019' [Graph]. *Statista.* URL: https://de.statista.com/statistik/daten/studie/320946/umfrage/ergebnisse-der-afd-bei-den-landtagswahlen/ [Accessed 5 November 2019].

Wehner, M. & E. Lohse (29 May 2016). '"Nicht als Nachbarn": Gauland beleidigt Boateng', *FAZ.* URL: www.faz.net/aktuell/politik/inland/afd-vize-gauland-beleidigt-jerome-boateng-14257743.html [Accessed 4 November 2019].

Welt (10 January 2018). *Einstweilige Verfügung gegen AfD-Politiker Maier.* URL: www.welt.de/politik/deutschland/article172355288/Halbneger-Gericht-erlaesst-Verfuegung-gegen-AfD-Mann-Maier.html [Accessed 4 November 2019].

ZDF (2 November 2019). *#Baseballschlägerjahre* [Video file]. URL: www.zdf.de/nachrichten/heute-plus/videos/baseballschlaegerjahre-rechte-gewalt-neonazis-100.html [Accessed 3 November 2019].

Index

Index

Index

Index

Index

Index

Index

Index